ONE HEART JUSTICE

CREATIVE CONTEMPLATION
FOR RADICAL CHANGE

K. BIRD

Note to Readers: The content and practices presented in this volume are designed for spiritual and creative experience and are not intended to replace professional mental health treatment.

Copyright @ 2024 Kristin Vitko

All rights reserved. No part of this book may be reproduced or used in any manner without the prior written permission of the copyright owner, except for the use of brief quotations in a book review.

To request permissions, contact the author at oneheartjustice@gmail.com

Paperback: 979-8-3507-2390-8

Ebook: 979-8-3507-2767-8

First paperback edition

Frist Ebook edition

Edited by Julia McNeal

Cover Art & Layout by Laura Boyle

One Heart Justice

In gratitude for all of life, past,
present and future.

CONTENTS

INTRODUCTION
Universal Energy for Healing and Change — 1

CHAPTER ONE
Fire – Temper Peace in your Heart — 27

CHAPTER TWO
Cosmos – Lead Through Interbeing — 51

CHAPTER THREE
Earth – Connect Through Healing Resonance — 72

CHAPTER FOUR
Water – Flow with Eternal Freedom — 96

CHAPTER FIVE
Air – Share Equity of Space — 120

CHAPTER SIX
Plant: Nourish One Another   144

CHAPTER SEVEN
Animal – Take Just Action   169

CHAPTER EIGHT
Light – Express Your Soul   192

WORKS CITED   212

INTRODUCTION

Universal Energy for Healing and Change

*"Black tribe, yellow tribe, red, white or brown,
From where the sun jumps up to where it goes down"*
                                        - Oodgeroo Noonuccal

This book is an invitation. I invite you to share this practice of heart-based living through creative contemplation called *One Heart Justice*. We focus on engaging in meditation, creative exploration and action to enliven our source of life energy and connect with eight universal elements as intelligent beings offering guidance and power to contribute to a more balanced and peaceful life on Earth. It is my hope that you have a transformational experience reading and participating in the practices at the end of each chapter both individually or with a small group. However you choose to experience this book, know that you are part of a community focused on learning, healing and collaborating to engage in creative change from the inside out.

Together we attune our hearts by listening to the source of life and to major aspects of creation. In so doing, we gain insight and cocreate visions of hope and healing for a better world. I share this meditative inquiry with you to join in the global dialogue centered on transforming human consciousness toward a world that works for all. We are united in values of integrity, equity, and heart-centered wisdom. Our strength as a community is in the multiplicity of places we live and the diverse, complex histories and perspectives we share. As we listen to know one another deeply, we practice interweaving global connections, focused on collaboration and reverence for difference.

One Heart Justice is inspired by young adults. I offer it to you, our young innovators, as a way of sharing what I have learned and to provide support in a way I was looking for when I was a younger person. As I write these words, I am middle aged and work with young people as a mental health and expressive arts therapist. It is deeply meaningful getting to know unique souls at the beginning of their journey. I find much of what young adults are searching for is their own capacity for wisdom and for others who will affirm this important aspect of humanity. It is my hope in offering this creative contemplation practice, to support you in your own soul searching, deepening into the truth of your inner wisdom, while also broadening your capacity for awareness and your presence of interbeing. May this practice provide guidance for listening to the fundamental components of life and focus you on your own unique contributions toward visions of a healing world.

MY PERSONAL JOURNEY

My earliest memories are of sitting among the trees and listening. I could hear the unique way the source of life speaks through all things. As I grew, I continued to have many experiences connecting me with what I can now describe as the presence of the unseen network within and beyond the physical realm we often refer to as the spirit world. I listened to my dreams, wrote poetry, followed symbols, and read works that resonated deeply with my heart and soul. As a young adult I became an Expressive Arts Therapist, and later, as a new parent, I began to meditate in earnest.

For most of my life I have grappled with depression and anxiety as well as my privilege as a white woman in America. I also identify as queer, which has positioned me to be open, experimental, unconventional, and searching. I have sought to integrate my openness to universal love and my education in psychology and other disciplines, with my capacity for intuitive ways of knowing, to contribute to making the world a thriving place for all. I have become more adept at seeing myself wholly, taking accountability, being self-forgiving, and forgiving others so that my heart can be open and expansive. I am more accepting of my blind spots, humble, and willing to learn, which gives me the courage to share my perspective here, in these pages.

The seeds for this practice were planted after the birth of my second child, when I began to meditate daily and felt called to journey, in self-guided meditation, to a sacred place in a forest where I would look up and the treetops formed a heart. This forest is within my imagination and yet it is connected to the physical realm in some way, and I wonder if one day I will find it on Earth. I journeyed to this spiritual forest in daily meditation over many years and had a variety of experiences that equipped me with transformative energy—for myself and the world around me. My daily meditation practice of various forms has allowed me to expand my heart, to attune to the vast interconnection of all that is, and to feel enlivened by the energy of creation. The personal growth I have experienced through this practice has given me clear guidance to explore the major components of life on our planet in new ways and to expand my experience of creation itself.

In this book I contemplate Fire, Cosmos, Earth, Water, Air, Plants, Animals and Light as conscious and intelligent entities, emerged from the source of oneness. I seek to honor peoples, cultures, and practices of the past and present that engage the natural world through contemplation, deep listening, creative illumination, and informed action.

As a Caucasian person living in the 21st century, I endeavor to take responsibility for the colonization and oppression of peoples who have stood firm in their wisdom of living with respect for each other and the world around them. The concepts and practices I offer in this work are intended to join with a global movement cultivating humanity's conscious reconnection with the natural world. This is one of many essential approaches of working together toward a better future for humans and a change in course for our planet.

Indigenous peoples around the world continue to practice traditions passed down through generations, designed to maintain balance and symbiotic development. This work seeks to be collaborative by engaging heart-based practice with nature while not co-opting specific practices of cultures that deserve protection, more resources and elevation in leadership.

The globalization of unsustainable practices driven by limited foresight, greed, fear, and hedonism have dominated the recent development of humanity. The time is now to move forward with a global shift in human progress through an awakening to the error of our ways and the reawakening of heart-based consciousness, inherent in all of us. We can each choose practices to increase empathy, respect, forgiveness, trust-building and peacemaking in our relationships with ourselves, one another, and all forms of creation on this planet we share. Collectively reweaving our relationships with all of life is the work of the heart that can lead us forward.

The more we make reparations, establish justice and trust, as well as prioritize and commit to healing our individual and collective trauma, the more capacity each generation will have to build on the best of human potential. As our collective wisdom deepens, so will our capacity to engage the present moment and our current lives with joy, love, and perseverance so that all beings may thrive.

I can sense children, a thousand years from the time I write this, calling back to me, guiding me down the path toward them. Their voices are illuminated by joyful wisdom and profound love, reminding me that we can work together for those to come. Each sacred step we take in this lifetime radiates out to those who will live far beyond this time. The children of tomorrow bring hope and visions for paths that lead to ways of living that are both ancient and modern with a foundation of harmony. If we listen, we can find one step after another toward this vision resounding with the depth of peace.

As you read these pages, I ask you to join me in having the courage to engage our radical imagination toward the creative transformation of mind, body, and spirit through attunement with the integrative and resonant source of life or Universal Heart. May we all continue to open our hearts and minds to further shift humanity toward balance and honor on our planet.

UNIVERSAL HEART

The concept and experience of the Universal Heart or Heart of Oneness is at the center of what we call divinity and can be thought of as the source interconnecting all things. Radiating out from the Uuniversal Heart, many theologies, paradigms and cultures have come and gone over the ages. The major religions of our time share, at their core, concepts that point to the Universal Heart, such as: eternal love, redemption; the values of integrity, respect, and compassion.

Over the course of history and in modern times, practices and institutions that begin as heart-centered, can stray from the source of love, becoming lost and twisted within the challenges of humanity. As we embrace the fact that each of us moves in and out of heart-based alignment daily, we can allow the branch of love called Forgiveness to bring us back into the source of life as eternal love. Together as we forgive ourselves and others we reconnect to the source of life and the radiance of universal love, so that we don't wander away too far and for too long from our true nature. We need each other's help to continue to cultivate a practice of heart-based living so that we can develop strong bonds of interfaith, intercultural, and international understanding and action. In this way, we will extend healing and collaboration beyond humanity and engage all of life with presence, respect, listening, and change.

ONE HEART JUSTICE

We have the opportunity to cultivate a collective way of being—the way of the one heart. This way of being is as old as humanity itself and yet profoundly connected to existence, held in our breath at this moment.

The wisdom and loving intelligence of the Universal Heart is a living presence connecting all things and can be attuned to through our own hearts in a myriad of ways. This attunement allows us to integrate our own hearts, minds, and bodies, and enables us to sense the presence, needs, and contributions of all things. Our physical hearts and energetic heart centers sense, synthesize, and guide us on a universal level. HeartMath Institute—a nonprofit organization conducting scientific research for over 25 years on the function of the heart—has determined that bringing awareness to the bioelectromagnetic connection between our own hearts, each other's hearts, and the Earth increases compassion, connection, and coherence.

The wisdom of the heart and heart-based practices have emerged in many diverse and beautiful ways including contemplative practices such as ritual, art making, storytelling, singing or chanting, and meditation. Neuroscientific research on the effects of singing, art making, and dancing together in groups points to the potential of syncing our hearts into coherent rhythms through creative collaboration. Attuning to life from our heart center places us in the context of interconnectivity and shifts us away from the drive for power over and into collective action.

A heart-based awareness is empowered by sharing love, which is accomplished through sensing, listening, understanding, and honoring so that we can know ourselves as the truth of beauty and collaborate with a sense of ease and flow. Science is revealing that the heart can sense events before they happen, demonstrating the potential of empathetic intelligence beyond time and space. Heart-based listening allows access to information from a broad range of levels of existence. Starting with the heart and radiating out in all directions, one can expand awareness to the edge of sensation and imagination, or, *sensamation*—toward a more full experience of all that is.

I believe the electromagnetic waves of the heart can attune to and vibrate in resonance with the consciousness of universal oneness, which I imagine as the frequency of love. I have learned this experientially, and in this book I invite you to practice heart-attunement, so that your own wisdom and connection are similarly ignited. Though I have a profound respect for science, I feel it is our responsibility to use our empirical experiences and intentions of unity to employ our spirituality and creativity toward healing our world, beyond what science can currently demonstrate. The human body experiences love energetically and neurochemically, becoming calm, alert, intuitive, and open to giving and receiving. When we choose to alight our own heart centers through awareness, we truly light up the world in attunement with the vibrational dimension of love as the fabric of the universe.

The intelligent knowing of my heart informs my mind that all is entrained in a universal whole.

I imagine the interplay of the quantum physics phenomenon, entanglement, in which particles connect over long distances and become part of the same system, inseparable. The tone of this wholeness is the voice of love, speaking multidimensional and infinite languages of diversity and oneness, in continuum. Heart intelligence guiding our intention and imagination cultivates our capacity to use meta-awareness for global healing.

ONE HEART JUSTICE

Fundamentally, we are created of subatomic spheres of vibrating microcosmic universal information. Through guided imagery, meditative states, dance, and other forms of spiritual artistry we can intentionally align our energy and awareness with the flow of interconnection often called the web of life. We can choose to resonate with universal love. And from this state of being, we engage life from a universal point of view, broadening our capacity to live dynamic, caring lives, finding humor in paradox and opening paths of creative possibility.

Many people and cultures have their own traditions and practices to enter this state of heart-based knowing, deeply rooted to the land they live on and their living histories. Let us take a moment to honor the heart-based cultures that have come and gone, many of whom have been killed by genocide or moved from their homelands across the globe. While no one culture we are aware of has achieved perfect unity, it is the intention and practice of heart based living with respect for all of life that has and will continue to move humanity closer to global peace. It is my hope that the more we each choose to practice heart-based living, the more protection and equity will be experienced by all peoples who have had their cultures and lands destroyed. Humanity owes deep gratitude to those who have and continue to protect, revitalize, and enliven heart-based practices in diverse forms. They protect endangered ecosystems and diaspora's while undergoing severe adversity to safeguard their ways of life and recover from hundreds of years of damaging practices by dominant cultures.

I believe it is our responsibility to each find ways to practice developing a consciousness of justice, unity, and peace, so that we contribute to a global shift in how we engage our world. I envision global systems based on a heart-based model and radical imagination that creates equity and mutual care. Taking time to engage in reverence for the immense diversity of humankind allows for awakened opportunities to regain balance with all of life.

Just as our breathing is giving and receiving, being and nonbeing, so is the origin and expansion of creation. Physics identifies subatomic particles, dark matter, and yet to be discovered aspects of the Cosmos as giving energetic form to the great expansive mystery. The source of spirit enlivening matter can be understood, in essence, as love. The miraculous interconnection of life-giving functions that created each one of us can be experienced as love. Love can be conceptualized as the orchestrating life force that creates and pervades all that is. I imagine that before the source of creation woke up to its own existence, perhaps creating the big bang(s), it was the void of nothingness only love could become. The simultaneous presence and expansion of love is awareness. Creation, it follows, is the imagination of awareness, born of love.

These are the visions I offer as you read through each chapter and engage in the *One Heart Justice* practice to have your own experiences. My hope is that each person finds what they most need through this contemplative process to grow in loving themselves and taking that love into action for a better world.

Engaging in contemplative practice, perhaps sitting in silence, one can begin to breathe full-body awareness into the field that unites all that is. From this place, what we call love can be thought of as the creative spiritual intelligence that allows all things to flow to and from one another. The pulse of life that transcends human existence blossoms into each physical form through love. As each person finds their way to engage with this field of interbeing and honors the spark of life in

ONE HEART JUSTICE

all things, we experience the unifying force of heart-based living. Together we strengthen this interconnected field through awareness and inspire one another. To be called to practice *One Heart Justice*, or any process embodying the Universal Heart is to have a direct experience and understanding of the intelligence that flows through all of life. Deepening our relationship with nature by using our neuropsychological ability to enter into intelligent communication with natural elements supports a shift in our conscious functioning toward giving each other and the natural world equal rights.

There are many ways to enliven one's experience of the Uuniversal Heart, passed down through the ages in various cultural, religious, spiritual, and familial practices. In this book, I endeavor to support you in practicing your own unique ways of expressing the universal spark of life and creative force of oneness. Once a path of attunement to the consciousness of the Universal Heart is established as a practice, we will begin to listen deeply to various bodies of creation. This is meant to be a deep, dynamic, transformative process, far exceeding guidance by the words that come through me. You are on your own path of wholeness, and this book is simply a conduit to conscious reconnection of your expression in reweaving a balanced world.

"Oneing" is an old English word that conveys the concept and practice of recognizing our connecting to all of creation. We can find practices of this nature in Buddhism, Hinduism, Islam, Christianity, Judaism, and all cultures with spiritual underpinnings as a way of experiencing the source of life and the interconnection of all things. While the narrative, nomenclature, and methods of oneing are diverse, the intentions are similar. Meditating with the intention of entering oneness consciousness we experience a nondual state of understanding, attuning to one source of life, and experience ourselves as part of this source. We then expand our awareness of the presence of source within all that exists. Oneing is important, because it dissolves all unnecessary barriers to uniting in shared reverence of life and generates profound empathy as we experience all that is other than ourselves as equal and unique manifestations of the source of life, beingness from which all emerges. As we practice oneing through the Universal Heart meditation, the sensibility of unity and nurturance begins to infuse our daily lives, allowing us to find openings where there were none before. A commitment to exploring the oneness of life naturally arises, and we find ways to connect to one another and the world in which we live through compassion, understanding, forgiveness, curiosity, restitution, and new ideas. Within embodied oneness, boundaries are created and held as space to protect ourselves and one another and cultivate safety for healing and growth, so that each being has space to thrive.

OUR SOULS AND THE UNIVERSAL SELF

The concepts of non being, source energy, soul and the universal self are central to the One Heart Justice process. All major religions and spiritual ways of life call us to the core of the heart as a gateway to the engagement and expression of the soul. I experience the soul as a unique composition of existence both separate in it's design, expression and evolution while simultaneously functioning in harmonious growth as part of the greater whole. I understand the soul to be the unique spiritual signature or unified consciousness enlivening each being; both individual and part of universal oneness. To experience the power and purpose of the soul we must shift from our cognitions and into a presence of embodied knowing. We sense the soul, we know when we are being soulful, when our souls are moved. The soul can begin to be understood as the deepest essence of our bodies and minds, both the entrance and exit of this manifestation in time and space. The soul is the deepest truth of ourselves; the essential consciousness of our individual selves that live on when our bodies die. This rich, vital body of knowing seeks the truth of interconnectivity and resonates with the souls of all beings with an innate understanding of the infinite and the one. The soul can be thought of as holding information or patterns of divine artistry from life time to life time, dimension to dimension in infinite wisdom. Attuning to our souls, the multidimensionality of existence may flourish and we can feel the eternal nature of the soul body both having traveled through other lifetimes on this planet and in formless states far beyond.

The wisdom of the soul, as part of the energetic matrix of the eternal finding its way back to the fullest experience of the universe, creates a sensorial path forward for humanity. As we follow the resonance of soulful knowing we continue to grow and evolve through the oneness we are a part of, sharing our unique expression through our temporal bodies within all that is.

Focusing on our individual sense of soul through somatic awareness we meditate to open our energy centers and engage the central axis running up and down our bodies to expand our soul energy and illuminate our interconnection with the web of life and experiencing our Universal Self. Practicing embodiment of the Universal Self engages us with oneness while allowing us to hold awareness of our individual selves, including our personal experiences and societal identities, while not being limited by these aspects of humanity and society. Through soulful connection with the Universal Self we can find both a sense of integrated responsibility in the here and now as well as an empowered sense of the eternal self. In the context of collaborative community justice work the Universal Self allows us to both take responsibility for our societal privileges as well as to heal damage to our sense of self caused by limiting beliefs and intersectional oppressive forces perpetuated by division and disconnection from oneness and equity. Each of us growing in our unique experiences and expressions practicing a heart based embodiment of Universal Self can keep us attuned to the goal of equity and protect us from getting stuck in guilt and/or hopelessness. Through this practice we each contribute what we are able toward a more equitable world while living within harmful and unsustainable societal systems.

The One Heart Justice process asks us to resonate with and explore the state of non being through somatic meditation to support the release of physical, emotional, and psychological energies or levels of consciousness that are not supportive of our soulful expression and create barriers to experiencing our Universal Selves. The concept and contemplation of non being helps us to attune with it's life giving paradoxical twin, the source of life. Dissolving toward non being allows us to release energetically and remerge through renewed life force energy to create resilience for our individual and communal lives.

This concept of emerging from a single source of life and the interconnection of all things through eternal love is embodied in the Universal Heart Meditation, the first step of the three-step expressive arts process *One Heart Justice*. I review all three steps below and at the end of each chapter you will connect to the source of all of life, and then employ this state of being to engage the major aspects of life, conceptualized as eight entities: Fire, Cosmos, Earth, Water, Air, Plants, Animals, and

Light. Engaging in the *One Heart Justice* process with each of these eight elemental forces, you will find guidance on how to channel universal energy to develop personal strengths for transformative justice.

WHAT IS ONE HEART JUSTICE?

Human cultures, over millennia and now, have developed ways to integrate the imagination, art, ritual, and spiritual sensibilities to collaborate toward healing and to enliven systems of wholeness. It is the integration of story, music, dance, and symbolic dress that have allowed humanity to stay connected to the natural world and aware of the spirit in all things. *One Heart Justice* is just such a practice.

My training as an Expressive Arts Therapist and my spiritual nature calls me to enliven heart-based wisdom through *One Heart Justice*, a creative contemplation practice that is both broad and distilled, to provide a universal space where all cultural and spiritual practices can meet.

One Heart Justice invites you to discover or continue your own ways of accessing, listening to, and expressing the consciousness of unity through contemplation and creativity. It offers opportunities to notice how you relate to yourself as a being of source energy, and to creativity as a means for vision, expression and radical transformation.

One Heart Justice as a creative contemplation practice is distilled into three experiential components. The steps are a guide for continuing to develop your own heart-centered life of love, creativity, and action. One Heart Justice can be practiced precisely or serve as inspiration to delve into your own creative process. It can be practiced both alone or with a group of trusted companions.

The first step of *One Heart Justice* is for you to engage in a Universal Heart Meditation to center and ground you in the source of creation and the interconnecting force of love. In this state of awareness within the universal web of life you can choose which aspect of creation to contemplate, such as Fire, Cosmos, Earth, Water, Air, Plants, Animals and Light, or you may wish to stay in a state of union with the Source of beingness or with nonbeing.

After you have chosen the focus of your creative contemplation, you engage in the second step of the *One Heart Justice* Process: Somatic Listening. This process entails bringing your awareness to your body sensations and emotional experiences and allowing yourself to hear them as words or see them as images. To recognize the element you are in contemplative dialogue with to speak to you through creative inspiration within your mind, heart, soul and body. Somatic Listening is a deep state of body-sensation-focused meditation in which you enter a dialectic process between your being and another state of consciousness. You will notice sensations in your body to explore through dialogue and movement, words to say or write down, sounds to make, art to draw or paint; trust your own being. You are a unique Self part of the Source of all selves, all beings. Allow your creative spirit to move you into expression in any way that feels right to you. Be open in a safe space to express.

The third step of the *One Heart Justice Process* is, Creative Exploration. This is when you shift into creative action translating and elaborating on your somatic experiences or body wisdom through artistic mediums such as movement, dance, writing, visual arts, sound and music or theater practices such as monologue or dialogue.

ONE HEART JUSTICE

TAKING CARE OF YOURSELF IN THIS PRACTICE

While engaging in meditation, body awareness, and the creative process, remember to listen to your own needs. If any experience feels like it is becoming too overwhelming or bringing up memories, images, or sensations that are not helpful for you, stop what you are doing and ground yourself in the present moment. Focusing on our internal experiences with attentiveness to the body can activate unresolved acute stress or trauma, and it is important you only engage with this material in a way that feels safe, helpful, and healing.

The *One Heart Justice* process also asks you to engage with powerful forces of life as individual entities which can bring up feelings of vulnerability and as an exercise in consciousness expansion can stimulate confusion or discomfort. If at any time during this practice you feel you are moving into experiences you need support with, take a break from the practice, integrate what you have learned and get support. You can go as slowly as you need to through each chapter, and it can also be helpful to create groups of friends to work through the *One Heart Justice* chapters together with for shared insight, inspiration and support. As a mental health therapist I encourage you to seek professional support if this practice or any other experience causes you to feel unsafe emotionally, psychologically, physically or spiritually.

THE ONE HEART JUSTICE PROCESS
Step One: Universal Heart Meditation
Visit Oneheartjustice.com for guided meditation recording of One Heart Justice process

To begin the Universal Heart Meditation, bring your whole body into awareness and allow whatever needs to dissolve into the void of nothingness, or nonbeing to release and fade away. Breathe into this dissolution state and relax into stillness, perhaps darkness. When you are ready, allow the source of life to emerge through your heart center and breathe deeply into your heart. As you exhale, know that you are in connection with the one source of all creation. Feel your heart spark with the intelligent life force causing it to beat. Allow the spark of life's source to alight in each of your energy centers moving up to your throat center, your third eye center, crown center and up above your head rooting into the source of life. Bring your awareness back down through each energy center and feel the spark of source life energy to blossom in your solar plexus center, your belly center, root center and down into your feet and below rooting into the source of life. Remember you are created of this one magnificent source, illuminating your heart, all of you, and all the innumerable manifestations of creation on Earth and beyond.

ONE HEART JUSTICE

From your radiant heart center, and all of your energy centers you can envision and feel this loving source intelligence radiating out from your body, until you are fully residing in a sphere of unconditional love. Stay here for a moment and soak in love as if you are a plant soaking in light.

As you experience the awareness of your whole body within the sphere of universal love, you can allow this energy to continue to expand in all directions, radiating further and further, as far as your sensory awareness and imagination will expand, until you know that you have expanded fully. Feel the love of the universe coming back toward you, enveloping your expansion in a hug, and know that you are fully interconnected with the web of life.

From this place, born of the source of all of creation and connected through the force of love, you can begin to listen, ask for guidance, share and receive information.

Step Two: Somatic Listening

When you are ready, you can move into Somatic Listening: listening with your full body by being mindful of sensations, images, words, cognitive impressions, and emotional tones within your body. We unify all the ways we receive information and communicate as sensory beings. In this way, Somatic Listening is a restful and receptive place of curiosity. It is a practice of being in whole body contemplation with the intention of receiving healing, wisdom, guidance, and inspiration. As you engage in Somatic Listening you can imagine your body is like a musical instrument being played by universal energy. As you notice body sensations, images, and emotions, you can choose to follow this sequence emerging or pause to take notes or sketch and then return to a meditative state and continue whole body listening. You may experience what I now call the *celestial ear*, a deep listening process in which you may hear language in the form of dialogue, poetic lines, or narrative form. Through the Somatic Listening process you are gathering the concepts, images, impressions, movements and words to elaborate through creative exploration and daily heart based practice. Devoting a journal to Somatic Listening will be helpful for documenting and conceptualizing how this practice will bring the most benefit to you.

Step Three: Creative Exploration

When you are ready, you can then move into the third aspect of the contemplation process, which is creative expression. The expressive arts medium that I chose for most of this book is contemplative writing, prose, and the creation of symbols embodying the spirit of each fundamental element of life. I have also been drawn to learning about the elements from a multitude of fields including: science, technology, education, design, and health practices. I believe in an integrated approach to cultivating the most mutually beneficial ways of living.

Your expressive arts practice can be in any artistic medium. It is not a matter of skill but of transformative experience. You may choose to take your sensory experience into movement, visual arts, sound or music. You can also choose for your creative expression to be focused on a problem you are solving, a current project, a relationship you are in process with or ideas of how to contribute your gifts to world. The wisdom you gain from your meditative experience is yours to create with in whatever way will best harness being in deep connection with the source of life and the elements that allow us as human animals to exist on the planet.

Make this experience your own as you move in and out of Universal Heart Meditation, Somatic Listening, and Creative

Exploration at your own pace. Be authentic to your own practice and allow your own artistry and methods to emerge.

Creation Myth

the void   nonbeing   absence of life
no thing
one can get close to it, almost disappear
until matter and antimatter awaken us
to the ever flowing expansion and contraction
that is breathing it all
invisible, like music
sounds, molecules, ideas, wonder
steady and still, present
simultaneously percolating
with patterns endlessly spiraling
in creative gestation

exponential as love from the center of the center of
nothing becoming
pushing the perimeter further into
what is not
fire weaving waves of light into matter
intertwining the nervous system of cosmos
emerging as living entity of unified diversity
a geometric paradox, flat and curved, holding us
together as we travel
quarks, protons, neutrons, atoms, stars, galaxies
transforming through space
cosmos, always becoming, scatters beings across
universe to remember where they came from
each creation, a matrix of the greater whole

Earth, it's inner core resonating with sun
source giving life with generosity of strength

ONE HEART JUSTICE

fiery formation erupting eons of volcanic mass
growing crust by cooled crust
heat as life radiates from Earth's center
shifting tectonic plates, creating
continents to crumble and reform
freezing and unfreezing
telling sedimentary stories for future reading
heat of charged particles riding electric currents
forming language of energy moving through
Earth to its edges and returning
interplanetary collision sending Earthen rock into
space, held close, our moon
reflecting soft light
saying, look at what we are a part of

from the drive of fire's perseverance
arises the gaseous form of water
water's vapors rise high
cooling to droplets forming clouds
dense with rain falling in trillions of drops
over millions of years
collecting in spaces of land
in motion to form oceans
full of chemical composure
replicating cycles of nourishment
water as current of life
collects and disperses, transporting growth
maturity of deep ocean and tempered steam
ascend from Earth's basin
achieving symbiotic creation
first single-cell common ancestor

growing, dividing, evolving
transmuting light into energy
proliferating oxygen
water becomes womb of life
giving rise to regeneration

at the interface of ocean, density lifts into gasses
growing in gravitational awareness
chemical compositions arrange themselves into
stratified spheres as air
oceanic circulation of spinning earth and equatorial
heat, the great messenger of
global tides, weather patterns, sound, wind
joining all in cycles of connection
allowing the atmospheric space to be, to listen
source of life in smallest form, microorganisms as
cyanobacteria in symbiotic symphony
water, sun and carbon dioxide
become photosynthesis
life blooms further as nucleus
is nourished into being
algae and seaweed swaying in oceans
bring more oxygen to air
complexity to cellular structure

plants grow onto land, mosses, liverworts, plants
with no names
spores spread, fertilization abounds, cell walls
strengthen, roots descend
from ferns, to conifers, to the first flower
plants thrive connecting earth, water, sun and air

ONE HEART JUSTICE

trees grow taller, forests form, ecosystems radiate
as wisdom of food, medicine
and shelter abounds
bacteria, viruses, and fungi force adaptation and
innovation to find balance
Earth's expression splits common ancestor onto
three distinct paths

animals emerge, from single-cell, soft-bodied
to multicellular vastness over billions of years
from sea worms and comb jellies
to trilobites and starfish, growth patterns and body
shapes adapt to habitats, creating shells, growing
spines, bridge from invertebrates to vertebrates
cycles of food and reproduction make flesh
bone and teeth
fish swim in, amphibians adapt, reptiles enlarge
mammals give live births, and insects infiltrate
from water to land and back to water
fossilized footprints leave clues to pursue the
puzzling mystery of evolution, cold-blooded and
warm-blooded, shaped and shaping environments

animals embody the soul of source, expressing
existence quadruped, biped, legless, finned
winged, animals nestling with Earth and elements
through evolution and extinction
ozone creates atmosphere, bringing us here
rodents, primates, hominids, shifting genes
DNA, chromosomes, all of us made of cells
a million times the number of stars in the

observable universe
hominid brains develop by listening, observing
learning to explore
homo sapiens advance enduring ways
over millions of years, solving problems
making tools, communicating, sharing knowledge
singing, growing larger
expanding across the globe
our greatest advancement in brain function
through adaptation to fast changing climates
we seek to survive
through countless cultures, from nomadic to
agrarian, discovering again and again
cooperation endures beyond brutality
love is innovative, all must thrive
for one to thrive

yet homo sapiens insist on separation for survival
tell each other stories of dehumanization
build on the backs of fellow humans
confuse propagation with progress
industrialize, using millions of years of
decomposition to damage the planet in decades
beyond repair for life as we know it
we continue to pollute, point fingers
make war and money to
further separate ourselves from
systems of truth, nature, our true nature
tearing each other down, twisting universal truths
into paradigms to convince each other
one way or another, the other is wrong

ONE HEART JUSTICE

how can this continue to happen when so many
seek peace, work tirelessly for justice
create beauty, forgive hundreds of years of
oppression, hold love at the center,
teach truths for a better world for all?

each of us holds this question
feeling the answer as an inner knowing
across the globe, building trust
forgiving ourselves, each other
merging ancient wisdom with modern discovery
we reweave our biome
in the best way for each of us pursuing gold of the
heart as vigorously as we have mined Earth
cultivating compassion, forgiveness, gratitude
trust and unconditional love
finding ways to heal ourselves, heal each other
regenerate our planet so that all may thrive
within each choice, each moment, we find unified
freedom through reverence for diversity
we open to the spectrum of life communicating
oneness, each being's light radiating their unique
expression of source here and now
knowing that when in hopeless struggle
we call darkness, we are held by light not yet
visible within the great expanse

primal light, first light
like being in the arms of the creator we imagine
which is us, loving ourselves, each other and all of
creation in this miraculous moment of duality

K. BIRD

between wave and particle
we breathe, we listen, we laugh, our bodies
instruments amplifying dynamic peace
restoring our planet and beyond the limits of our
collective imagination
Earth vibrating with such intensity
our families in the stars call out
Hurrah!
each of us, when we are ready, riding into
initial singularity
and out again

ONE HEART JUSTICE

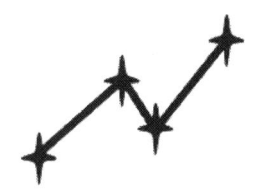

CHAPTER ONE

Fire – Temper Peace in your Heart

"I am the throat of the sandia mountains"

— Joy Harjo

Fire alights the metaphoric molecules of the human spirit and mirrors the source of all things through its eternal burning. Often, we experience the spirit of Fire through compassion and resilience in our darkest moments. To begin developing a relationship with Fire beyond what you already know; allow the sensation of warmth to permeate your body and open you to the mysteries of Fire as a fundamental entity of creation, bringing knowledge to humanity.

Getting to know Fire as a spiritual entity, as well as a physical manifestation, we recognize it is not simply flame, but also the potential for flame teaching us about the nature of possibility. In meditation with Fire today, I feel it's guidance to sense this potential in all things as the opportunity for peaceful transformation. Fire acknowledges it's propensity for destruction and offers that restoring justice sustainably requires the least use of force and violence. Forming a relationship with Fire as an ally in cultivating balance for all of life it asks us to sense it's presence in a way that feels safe for each of us and to begin to recognize it's signature energetic presence during contemplative practice.

As humans experiencing the Fire of our sun, it is not hard to imagine how dependent we are on Fire, physically. Just as our planet rotates and we experience being closer to and further away from the sun, so too, our relationship with Fire can be distant or intense. As a Universal spirit Fire has physical, psychological, emotional, and spiritual aspects. It exists in these forms as an invisible presence, a spark, a single flame, and can become a raging inferno or massive explosion of immense power. Deepening a relationship with Fire, it is important to develop one's internal discipline and temperance. Contemplating Fire from a soul-based perspective will help us to manage our internal Fire and respect Fire's capacity for destruction, pain, and transformation. Fire reminds us peace is created by the temperance of our own rage toward injustice and to channel this anger as a burning drive to stand in truth that reveals just action.

Exploration of Fire draws us back into its role in human evolution, just as it propels us forward into it's expansive presence as part of galactic phenomena. Fire imagines the beginning of

ONE HEART JUSTICE

the Universe as the possibility of the Big Bang, while it also invites mysteries that remain to be discovered about universal creation. Fire can be experienced as a gateway—a path between the physical and ethereal realms of existence.

Collectively, we look into the face of potential extinction through an atmospheric shift with the warming of our planet. It is a good time to focus on learning from our ancestors and current cultures that have revered Fire and understood it as an entity to be explored in its fullest range and capacities.

As I begin to bond with Fire in expanded ways, I find it is necessary to have courage. Fire is power, and I am careful not to underestimate it as I invite its presence more fully in my life. I cultivate temperance in meditation with Fire by shifting from fear to curiosity. Meditating with Fire as my focus, shows me two places in my body where imagining heat can be beneficial at this moment to feel more grounded, able to sustain and create.

In the Northern Hemisphere, where I live, it is Fall as we tilt further from the sun; leaves turn warm shades, allowing light to shine through them and glow. I soak in their beauty and begin to glow from the inside out, feeling deeply connected to nature around me. The sun warms my skin on this clear Fall afternoon, and I feel grateful for its waning presence. I feel part of the orchestration of Fire, and, listening to it, feel it's presence all around me. It is the great conductor of life: growing plants, cooking, transporting us, moving electricity and information. Fire reminds me that as humans come to know it more fully as an intelligent entity we can further understand how to make human systems operate without overheating the planet or contributing to overmining for resources.

Just as life on Earth is becoming more challenging for humanity, I sense Fire's awareness that it is becoming an increasingly damaging force. Fire speaks loudly in its destruction as global warming increases and mass wildfires escalate, globally. Fire waves itself brightly, saying, *learn to work with me,* and reminds humankind of our responsibilities having such an influential presence on this planet. Fire calls us to integrate all our functions of intelligence, mind, body, intuition, and logic when interacting with Fire, in the very same way that Fire itself emerges, through the interaction of multiple elements. Bringing our full capacity to exploring its nature and developing an intimate relationship with Fire, we unlock our own potential to manage Fire in all it's forms and enliven it, and ourselves, with grace and ease.

Engaging Fire on a psychological, emotional, and spiritual level, I wonder about what it means to have a burning passion: passion for another person; passion for justice; passion for teaching. From this perspective, what is the *material* that is burning, the chain reaction that creates a fiery disposition and creative transformation? I hear Fire saying spiritually, it burns the substance of truth—truth as whatever concept, situation or object is expressing the eternal source of life. The heart that burns with passion is the heart that is emitting the truth of unconditional love. When the mind burns with the passion of ideologies separate from the heart of truth, danger ensues. To understand the metaphysical nature of Fire burning invisibly and making itself visible through physical flame, is to understand the element of Fire as radiant eternal presence and as a tool for transformation on all levels.

Fire shows me the peaceful flame flickering elegantly, reminding us all is well. Fire asks us to consider what we need from its capacity and to continue to teach one another how to use it in ways that will not harm other forms of life. The simple candle flame symbolizes the one source of life, and the peace of knowing all is connected through the universal flame as a vehicle for unconditional love. Fire guides us to understand the singularity of stillness and molecular transformation within the candle flame as a symbol for our own positioning as those seeking a just world.

Fire is energy. Archeologists study the origin of Fire in the evolution of humanoids, and as we imagine our earliest relationship with Fire, we connect to the roots of our existence. To imagine a time when all we had were the tools we discovered in nature is to recall a time during which humans had no opposing concept to nature. Humans are exemplary in our capacity to create realities through the stories we tell ourselves, individually and collectively. Developing a narrative that creates a more intimate relationship with Fire is an opportunity to ground ourselves in one of the most important relationships we can have as animals. To get back to the basic components of Fire and how it has evolved opens channels for Fire itself to guide us. Spending time outside, getting wet, being cold, brings us directly in contact with the physical necessities of Fire for our survival.

We can open our hearts and our minds to hear the voice of Fire in our most technologically advanced cityscapes and human projects. When I tune into Fire as an entity, from a global perspective, I hear it calling for the reining in of flagrant human conflict.

Conflicts that flare across the globe through actions of war, as well as internal conflicts, can and must be harnessed at a very personal level. When pursuing the path of the radiant heart, the source of oneness reverberates out diametrically. To innovate solutions that emerge from conflict in the most compassionate and equitable ways is to contribute to peaceful radiance. We look to the practice of reconciliation, dousing the threat that flares with listening, understanding, and forgiveness. We temper existential demise with the trust and care we show in our relationships, beginning with the relationship we have with ourselves. The practice of cultivating a relationship with Fire is connected to the practice of finding peace within oneself and to join in restorative justice when the rage of injustice threatens to burn—through violent revolution, more than is necessary—to the ground. To fight Fire with Fire is a practice that leads to total destruction and can be connected to a drive for competition of "power over." To collaborate with passion for the betterment of all is the torch guiding us as we understand Fire as a component of our own bodies, minds, and souls.

As I listen to Fire for guidance, I hear Fire saying we are burning too much on all levels of existence. In the psychological realms, we are too driven by competition and conflict which needs to be balanced by collaboration and peace-making. In the physical realms we are burning too much fossil fuel and taking down too many trees, along with many other damaging practices, and need alternative systems of energy—as well as planting and protecting forests. Fire recognizes that humanity is stuck in patterns that are destructive due to fear for survival and clinging to ways of life that are limited by current structures of human power and consciousness locked into global economic systems. Fire asks us to find the courage to let go of what we know and make a leap into imagination and desire, to create a world that will not only work for all of humanity, long-term, but for all of life.

Fire guides us through the warmth of our hearts to cultivate the redistribution of power through everyday acts of love, by listening to one another and the very elements of life itself on the planet. Fire inspires us, through it's steady glow, to take one step at a time to change these systems in time for life to continue in a symbiotic way, and to further enhance and grow in fullest potential through collaborative restoration and shared passion.

I ask Fire about the pain and loss it causes and the grief that ensues. Fire asks us to support one another to find strength as we collaborate for greater balance. It reminds us anger and grief can be perceived as processes of burning transformation, through love and loss, shifting our internal and external landscapes. The deep pain of grief has the capacity to open us to greater compassion, as heartbreak not only hurts but enlivens the sensitivity of the feeling heart. Fire understands it causes irrevocable damage and asks for forgiveness as it offers itself as an ally in generating solutions to minimize suffering and maximize resilience, joy and peace.

Fire is the expression of truth bringing us to our core, to the source of all things expressed in each moment. The Source of life flows as Universal Love through the element of Fire, warming our heart centers like an ember glowing with the balance of breathing out, letting go and inhaling the here and now. From our hearts warmed by the passion of Fire we find acceptance and patience for difficult processes and integrity for ourselves and others.

Embracing Fire in the body, mind, and soul allows us to dissipate illusion and distraction, and collectively can allow us to become clear on what is essential. When we join together, through the most real aspects of ourselves in the moment, we allow for the letting go of systems that are not providing equity on a cultural, societal, and global scale. Connecting with one another from the core of our humanity will allow us to connect with what is most important on micro and macro levels—in our relationships with ourselves, with others, with housing, food, health care, education, and transportation. The spiritual truth burning of Fire brings us closer to the truth of what sustains us and all aspects of life.

Experiencing a deepened and expanded relationship with Fire can be challenging, because Fire burns away our false egos, our defenses, the limitations of worthiness placed on us by outdated forms of thought and internalized in ways that are not helpful for improving the sustainment and flourishing of interdependence. This process can be likened to that of the Firewalker. The Firewalker goes through a psychological, spiritual process of letting go of fear and embracing the effects of Fire. We don't have to be able to walk on Fire in the physical realm to arrive at this core understanding, but the metaphor of releasing fear and embracing acceptance is effective. Knowing that as we let go and allow Fire to transform us through contemplation, we become bound to it through loving connection and grounded in a slow, peaceful burn.

Imagining Fire as an expression of the source of life burning eternally, we are invited to bring it into our hearts to radiate peacefully. We both emit this source Fire and receive it in physical form. I receive it as light from the sun and reflect on the sun's power to facilitate growth and change. My skin and my eyes absorb sunlight, metabolizing and creating that which I need for my body to function. I also recognize that too much sun can be harsh, and I need to shield myself and limit exposure. As we respect Fire, we learn to honor each being's needs and limits, to cultivate a nourishing relationship with one another.

I consider people who know Fire intimately in their work, and those who have been directly affected by Fire—such as firefighters, people who specialize in fire safety, and people who have been deeply harmed by fire—and I wonder what they have learned. I feel compassion for the trauma people endure through Fire and send them hope for continued healing. I ask Fire about the trauma it causes and for its guidance on how to heal from those wounds. Fire brings my awareness to the human body and the excruciating pain burns cause, and to those who have experienced intense grief due to losing loved ones, homes, animals, and forests to Fire. For healing, Fire offers hope for continued communal learning in how to innovate medical technology for physical healing as well as psychological, emotional and spiritual techniques for restoring health. Fire asks us to relearn methods for forest restoration and management to allow vegetation to return to scorched earth to utilize housing and community development strategies that protect us from Fire and Fire from it's destructive aspects.

For psychological and emotional trauma caused by Fire, it also shows me the choice of forgiveness. It acknowledges the hate, fear, and devastation it causes and asks to be an ally in the forgiveness process. Fire understands each being must forgive in its own time and way, and shares that it can help us find the essential gift of truth, gained from our most painful experiences, as we forgive ourselves, others and Fire itself. Fire shows me how the process of forgiveness can feel like warm embers of compassion, burning away the emotional energy of hate, blame, powerlessness, revenge, and disempowerment. Holding ourselves with the warmth of self-compassion allows us to endure these painful feelings toward ourselves and others that have harmed us. Fire shares that each of us, if and when we are ready, can extend compassion allowing for a release—a letting go and a transformation. The forgiveness process Fire teaches us through the spirit of compassion opens our hearts to new learning, growth, and understanding, grounded in the core truths it has revealed. Fire emphasizes that the forgiveness process doesn't happen all at once; it is a choice we make each moment it feels right.

Fire understands: in its physical form it can be traumatic, destructive, and deadly, and I hear it saying it wants to be in more balance. It does not want to be destructive to its fellow beings, to destroy entire ecosystems, to burn in ways that are polluting. Fire seeks to be restored to its own wise functioning and asks humans to begin to attune to their own innate wisdom in relation to the elements of life. To restore our collective role as wisdom keepers of Fire is to begin acknowledging Fire as a living presence. Fire says it does not mean it will not flare out of harmony and harm at times, but that when it does, more focus can be placed on how to heal this area to minimize that harm. Fire feels out of control on Earth, wants to cause less harm, and wants to be a greater force of creativity and regeneration. Fire needs our help to make this happen by increasing our awareness of and connection to it daily.

We look for Fire in our modern world and expand it: from the fireplace, the campfire; from our understanding that it is the living power that emanates from our light bulbs, our water heaters, computers, and cars as well as an aspect of our very beings. We feel Fire, and we come to respect it from a place of love rather than fear. We cultivate a healthy respect for Fire and in so doing, release our fear of change. We allow structures of power related to the resource of Fire and fuel to shift, in direct conversation with the living force of Fire, listening for what it requests.

Holding reverence for Fire will provide the most enduring systems of life for humanity. With regard to continued life on

ONE HEART JUSTICE

Earth, Fire asks us to deepen our understanding of wisdom itself. Wisdom is the ability to open one's heart and mind, body and soul, to another; to have mutual respect as beings sharing information and differing perspectives. Wisdom broadens one's own perspective beyond the individual experience and into the greater realm. It offers ways of preserving our bodies and protecting us as well as allowing for our exploration and interconnection of information between peoples and cultures.

With wisdom, we are called to recognize we are misusing Fire in ways that now threaten the entire planet. Fire says the shift is to understand how to innovate our current relationship with it to offset the damage we have created. Fire says revolution happens within our hearts and minds, and the solutions and systematic changes necessary are simple and elegant—and in many forms, already exist. From a scientific perspective, we know how to store the heat of Fire, and, Fire says, there are many gentle ways to tap into the heat of Fire within the Earth that maintain the integrity of ecosystems.

New ways of getting what we need from Fire through enhancing our relationship with the natural world is an expression of love. Love is expansive and opens space for connection, understanding, and innovation. To approach the element of Fire from a place of love allows more information, more collaborative ideas to permeate our current collective understanding. The restoration of wholeness, to forgive ourselves, to forgive those that have harmed us, allows us to feel ourselves yet again as part of a much larger living system. We thrive best in a cohesive position rather than in a state of opposition—in which nature, Fire, other human beings, other animals, are not our enemy. Humans can continue to protect ourselves and live in relative comfort, and innovate in a way that is beneficial for all of life. To give other creatures their space and right to co-exist, knowing that there will be edges in which life is lost. Fire says those experiences can be minimized. It is necessary to restore Fire as a great teacher of truth and balance to learn the nature of peace within diverse transformation.

Today, as I experience my own grief and rage, I wonder what Fire has to teach me about moving forward. I sit in stillness, feeling intense emotional pain in my body, and listen for Fire's response. Fire shows me how to accept pain as information shifting my internal experiences, my understanding and awareness. Fire reminds me that allowing and being present with emotional pain creates more space for transformation. I sink into feeling defeated, afraid, and hopeless—this is the darkness. With the wisdom of Fire, the quality of darkness changes from ominous to originating. I am back at the beginning, the fertile empty space. My pain dissipates, and I am in a field of potential where Fire as creative spirit glitters with possibilities. This is how burning and regeneration are inexorably connected. I have all I need internally to be present to life unfolding.

I thank Fire for its giving, as I listen to the heater in my home warming the rooms and feel the lights glowing where I sit writing by the cold blue dusk of winter sky. I wonder, how do I know this is Fire guiding me, and do we each have different experiences of the same aspects of life? Where are the lines between what I sense as the spiritual force of Fire and my own imagination? I wonder what is the function that allows me to hear and to feel guidance when I reach out for answers? Is it possible to integrate this way of knowing with modern scientific principles? Is it helpful to cultivate a deep spiritual connection with Fire and other elements of nature and to encourage others to do the same?

ONE HEART JUSTICE

The one source of universal love reminds me: Fire lights the way for me in this moment of questioning, and although it seems a most destructive force at this time on the planet, in the face of global warming it in fact continues to hold much promise for collaboration.

As I sit for my daily meditation with Fire, I ask what it is Fire wants me to know so that I can be a better human being on the planet and also share with others. Fire brings my attention to how I know that it is the presence of Fire itself I am in contemplation with. Fire brings me to my heart as the place in my body that I open to the broadest experience I currently have with the source of all things, the one flow of life. The essence from which Fire and I both emerge helps me to hone in on Fire as having a certain tone in my body, a sensation that allows me to experience a knowing: it is the presence of Fire. There is a particular way I receive Fire's guidance, a familiar connection.

Through relationships we become familiar with the feeling of the other, and the feeling we make together. I think of the sensations I have when I communicate with Fire; a steady sensation of warm humming. From this heart-centered communication, I feel Fire asking me to trust it.

I share with Fire that I feel like an infant in my understanding of how it works—how to make a Fire without modern assistance in the form of matches, even having wilderness training on using flint and tinder bundles. Yet, I have no confidence in creating Fire on a moment's notice or understanding of how Fire becomes electricity or combusts to start a motor. I ask Fire: how can I help to innovate and be a steward of Earth through getting to know you better if I personally am so lacking in understanding of our current technologies? Fire reminds me that it is true we all have our gifts and contributions to share. The practice of deepening our emotional, psychological, physical, and spiritual connection with the elements of life can help others to hone their own gifts in ways that are true to the essence of love; we can interconnect and create a place where sustainable technology is infused with soul and wisdom.

Fire again reminds me of the eternal flame as a guide to sustaining hope with an even, steady vision toward unwavering progress. Fire reminds me that even when the light is dim, there's hope. When the Fire of sudden passion and transformation ignites and there is a major victory, the seed of hope is always at the heart. Fire grants me the vision of a world at peace and reminds me that those aspects of self that are afraid to engage in the seeming utopian naivety of such a vision are really the aspects of self that would do well to be warmed with love. The fuel of love, turned inward, allows us to have the courage to walk daily with this vision of peace on Earth. To hold this vision of peace on Earth in one's heart is necessary, even in the face of being perceived as naive, foolish, weak, or unrealistic.

Fire reminds me that true courage and sustainable motivation are derived from the one source of love, and that this is not a truth that can be proven necessarily, because our perception of truth is a matter of the integration of our dedication, openness, generosity, and relationship with the world around us. Fire reminds me that to sustain this hope one must be anything but naïve: One must allow the realities of tragedies and injustices across time and the globe to permeate the body and soul; allow the utmost pain to open one's heart with empathy, resilience and hope; and to commit with fortitude to the practices that take us one step closer to vision. It is possible to keep one's feet on the ground, firmly planted in the reality of the current day and age, while also opening to all that has come

ONE HEART JUSTICE

before and all that is to come, and at the center, finding the one, still place where love was born. It is a gift to be given a vision, a felt reality of the possible future where peace, balance, respect, and love prevail.

I ask Fire, what am I—a person who is simply meditating and listening with an open heart to contribute? Fire responds that it is essential to reconnect with elements and aspects of life in this way in order to integrate modern human development with an absolute, rooted connection to the natural world. Fire says it is necessary to increase our reconnection to the wisdom traditions that are carried in our physiology and that have been carried on culturally by peoples who have been persecuted and oppressed. Many of these cultures have been destroyed or greatly damaged and yet continue despite modern pressure, because these truths cannot be fully lost. I answer, that I honor current cultures who have carried on these sacred ways of relating to our world, and I seek to practice from a universal perspective so as not to co-opt any specific cultural traditions. In this way, it is the heart of sacred interconnection that is embodied to empower the collective. Fire reminds me again of the collective—that many people hold these understandings and ways of being in their heart and yet are forced to repress them by our current societal structures and logic heavy systems. No one, individual choice can change global trends that are leading humans further from a sustainable world for all creatures on the planet.

This evening, I feel the intimacy of Fire all around me, smoldering underground, reflecting off the moon in the evening light and ask, how does my individual calling to communicate with the world in this way relate to my relationship with my children, as they are influenced by me yet swept along by the culture of entertainment, comfort, and possessions? Our children learn from our priorities—our right actions—and observe us relating to the world around us. They can hear it in the way we say the word, Fire, the way we relate to the sun, the way we teach them about the resources of the planet. They feel the respect we have for and understanding of the sentient spirit and interconnectivity of Fire and of all of life on Earth and beyond. I wonder how to continue to guide my children to feel into this way of relating to Fire; to the world? Fire shows me: to be the living presence of heart-based interconnection as much as possible and my children soak it in.

In contemplation with Fire I am brought again to the metaphor of the molecular interactions that create combustion and the emergence of physical fire. Fire draws me to consider this phenomena from a range of perspectives, including the opportunities created through interdisciplinary collaboration with a focus on equity among all people, all *beings*, and sustainable engagement of resources. Fire reminds me that integrating social justice, economics, art, science, and education among other fields, toward the intention of an equitable, healthy planet provides interactions that create new ideas and enlighten us with new possibilities. Integration requires openness, listening, creativity, and acceptance, yet even with these skills, conflict ensues. Just as when molecules come together to create fire there is friction, integration, and change, this also causes conflict. Fire teaches that if one endures conflict with respect and establishes trust, something new can be created. It is a fruitful practice when conflict ensues in my country, in my partnership, between my children, with colleagues. I remember we're not trying to change the other, but can simply create something new by listening, accepting, and collaborating. There is an openness that comes from deep respect from the innermost

ONE HEART JUSTICE

regions of the fiery passion of the heart and soul to create new ways of being.

Fire teaches us good boundaries to keep ourselves safe as trust and respect are established and maintained. Fire shows us how an environment of safety can help us come together to serve one another. This capacity to heal conflict, right wrongs and restore equity and health is an area humans must put more effort into, both individually and collectively. Through introspection, contemplation, and devotion to a deep sense of peace, we increase our ability to love ourselves—including our most hidden, vulnerable, and hateful parts. It is through this deep internal work, with support of others, of our communities, we can then face one another and move toward healing.

Fire reminds me of the Cretaceous-Tertiary extinction, when the asteroid hit Earth, leading to a mass extinction of three quarters of the plants and animals on the planet. A current theory holds that when the asteroid hit, it sent particles of Earth into the atmosphere, and in their burning return to the Earth, due to gravity, created an incredibly hot atmosphere. The atmosphere became too hot for most of the current lifeforms to survive. Fire warns me, we are moving toward that level of extinction, and we have a choice: to work with one another and the elements of life on Earth in new ways to prevent this from happening. Fire asks us to remember its participation in the creation of our planet in its molten state. To imagine how it creates mountains and shifts the landscape through molten lava under tectonic plates. Fire reminds me of its contribution in the formation of stars, the ordering of galaxies and aspects of life forms, beyond what we currently know.

As we feel close to Fire, we feel Fire within us as part of who we are, part of our bodies, our souls, and spirits. As we feel Fire in our daily lives, our world, the creation of where we live, Fire asks us to remember its expanded understanding of the universe itself. In connecting with the Fire we cultivating the vast richness of Fire's capacity, in a cosmic sense. We can feel that expansiveness within ourselves as we percolate with possibilities and the courage to create new things, while being grounded in the very sacred origin of our lives. Fire calls for each of us to share our authentic voice burning in the truth of the moment. Fire casts its glow on each of our faces—just as we blow out candles on a birthday, each of us is celebrated, nurtured, and engaged as who we truly are. We each deserve equal resources and shared opportunities. Fire dances in celebration of diversity, from the most authentic inner connection, allowing for conflict between differences to create the reverence, respect, and safety that we each deserve. In this way, new landscapes form, such as governing ourselves from a sustained approach; equity and respect can emerge.

Fire says that in the dynamic of change, when it becomes too much to express love, respect, and safety to one another other and we begin to lash out in harm, we can practice containing our anger and practice love, respect, and safety. Opportunities for listening, understanding, and working together arise, one conversation at a time, loving self and other new landscape forms emerge. Dynamic change through the process of love, Fire says, can transform the ways we govern our individual selves, and how we engage in concentric circles—with our families, communities, nations, and the Earth itself. From our micro moments, of tending our own wounded hearts; to our macro visions of greater global harmony, these are the teachings that we can find in all of life.

When it comes to trust, Fire says that the metaphor of metal arts is demonstrative—using the presence and guidance

ONE HEART JUSTICE

of Fire in understanding and establishing trust with ourselves, others, and all that is. The burning of the heart, full of the activity and openness of love, is like molten metal. The function of heartbreak, pain, grief, and betrayal is to transform the heart and soul as well. This is the alchemy of transmuting pain to establish a wider and deeper trust with all that is. The transformative power of intense love and intense pain puts us in a permeable state, in which we can fortify connection to the source of life and eternal flow of freedom.

I ask Fire to guide me in the moments when bonds are betrayed to alchemize pain by enduring intensity and cooling our internal and relational friction with acceptance. Acceptance takes the oxygen out of hate and allows us more energy for compassion directed at ourselves and others. Fire says we can be restored by deep inner work and soulful insights, by keeping ourselves and each other safe and finding courage to explore new connections again when ready. Fire points us to community to help heal the wounds of broken trust—to the practice of supporting and reestablishing trust for our fellow beings; that will take us in the direction where trust will be less often breached on a broad scale. Through this resilience process, we establish a very firm trust with ourselves, those who support us, and life itself.

Fire reminds us that as an element on an Earth causing destruction in ways that can be altered by humanity, it is our responsibility to bring balance back to the planet. Among humanity itself, many peoples are being forced to carry the load—suffering loss of lives, health, and dreams. Fire shows us that all of life suffers when we do not choose to walk the path of mutual nourishment for humanity and all of life. Fire offers the image of lighting one another's candles as we come together to sooth one another's mourning as well as to celebrate our accomplishments. Fire calls us to celebrate each other's gifts as the spark of co-creation, igniting the wildfire of radical hope.

Fire reminds me of what we've learned about gratitude, and says to think about gratitude as a way of finding strength by amplifying beauty, joy, and vitality. Gratitude shifts the burning of life from being damaging to being life-giving in our awareness. Fire shares its honor as a giver and keeper of light through combustion of love, pain, and truth. Fire reminds us that from love and pain comes the fire of creation.

I thank Fire for lending support for forging practices of forgiveness and restitution of trust, toward healing deep wounds, so that humans may work more closely together for the good of all for greater peace. Fire shows me how we keep our own and each other's internal flame or motivation going so that we may be warmed by seeking beauty and inspiration, accepting care from others, experiencing interdependence, with heart-based listening and understanding.

It is interesting to think about Fire as making its own choices. Could Fire decide not to burn down a forest, a home, or take a life? I hear Fire saying, all of life in physical form can only use our will as much as the environment allows. Fire reminds us we are so interconnected it only has the capacity to maneuver itself in physical form as much as human hearts and minds have considered its presence in the safest, most beneficial capacity. Fire will deeply transform in a way that feels more in harmony with the fabric of our existence if it is understood and worked with in a way that acknowledges its function, power, and wisdom as a fundamental intelligence of the source of life. The element of Fire is intrinsically connected to the care that is taken to keep it in balance.

ONE HEART JUSTICE

Fire says it has the potential to be least harmful and most beneficial when nourished in its existence through the hearts of humanity. Fire also reminds us of our mortality and acceptance of the natural limitations of our own flesh. Fire asks us to surrender to spiritual and psychological transformation, and to resonate with Fire as a beautiful force within and among us. Fire asks us to consider the broader system of the living universe, far beyond our individual lives.

At the interface of our internal, spiritual Fire and the physical use of Fire in our current world, what is it that Fire can offer us in a new way if we engage Fire in direct communication? How do we at once relate to Fire as necessary for life itself, as we know it, while also integrating the technologies and comforts we have innovated, without losing the direct connection to what it is we're working with? Fire says in this moment to be grateful for what we have learned and continue to be open to innovations inherent in connecting with the direct intelligence of Fire.

ONE HEART JUSTICE PROCESS
Universal Heart Meditation

Visit Oneheartjustice.com for guided meditation recording of One Heart Justice process

To begin the Universal Heart Meditation, bring your whole body into awareness and allow whatever needs to dissolve into the void of nothingness to release and fade away. Breathe into this dissolution state and relax into stillness. When you are ready allow the source of life to emerge through your heart center and breathe deeply into your heart. As you exhale, know that you are in connection with the one source of all creation. Feel your heart spark with the intelligent life force causing it to beat. Allow the spark of life's source to alight in each of your energy centers moving up to your throat center, your third eye center, crown center and up above your head rooting into the source of life. Bring your awareness back down through each energy center and feel the spark of source life energy to blossom in your solar plexus center, your belly center, root center and down into your feet and below rooting into the source of life. Remember you are created of this one magnificent source, illuminating your heart, all of you, and all the innumerable manifestations of creation on Earth and beyond.

ONE HEART JUSTICE

From your radiant heart center, and all of your energy centers you can envision and feel this loving source intelligence radiating out from your body, until you are fully residing in a sphere of unconditional love. Stay here for a moment and soak in love as if you are a plant soaking in light.

As you experience the awareness of your whole body within the sphere of universal love, you can allow this energy to continue to expand in all directions, radiating further and further, as far as your sensory awareness and imagination will expand, until you know that you have expanded fully. Feel the love of the universe coming back toward you, enveloping your expansion in a hug, and know that you are fully interconnected with the web of life.

From this place, born of the source of all of creation and connected through the force of love, you can begin to listen, ask for guidance, share and receive information.

Hold the spirit of Fire in your heart, your mind, and your body. Be present with whatever arises. As always, if this feels uncomfortable, you may try shifting from fear to curiosity. If you begin to feel overwhelmed in any way, take a break from the practice and engage in self soothing and getting support. When contemplating Fire feels right, continue into Somatic Listening.

SOMATIC LISTENING

As you move into Somatic Listening and listen with your whole body by being nonjudgmentally aware of body sensations, images, words, cognitive impressions, and emotional tones, imagine these are ideas allowing you to learn with Fire. If you lose focus, bring your awareness back to you heart center and smile, feeling the presence of Fire in your heart as you breathe and regain focus. Notice what sensations, images, emotions, and words draw your attention most and feel powerful to explore further. Ask Fire what messages it has for you to deepen your understanding of tempering peace through your heart center. As you hone in on impressions to transition into creative exploration with, take a moment to make notes or draw in your journal, or amplify body sensation into movement, or sound. Use whatever ways seem most effective to bring expression and understanding to your Somatic Experience with Fire that is the right way for you today.

CREATIVE EXPLORATION

As you move into the third aspect of the creative contemplation process, Creative Exploration, know that you can return to the Universal Heart Meditation and Somatic Listening at any time, and then back into Creative Exploration.

Your expressive arts practice can be in any artistic medium. You may choose to take your sensory experience into movement, visual arts, sound, or music. You can also focus on a problem you are solving, a current project, a relationship you are in process with and ask Fire to support you with new approaches and ideas. The wisdom you gain in contemplation with Fire is yours to create with in whatever way that is best for you.

Make this experience your own as you move in and out of Universal Heart Meditation, Somatic Listening, and Creative Exploration at your own pace. Be authentic to your own practice and allow your own patterns and methods to emerge. Begin to notice in every day life how Fire is present in all of it's forms and how you can sense it as an intelligent force that is familiar in it's connection to your mind, body, and soul.

CHAPTER TWO

Cosmos – Lead Through Interbeing

"We need the stars…We need purpose! We need the image, the Destiny, to take root among the stars gives us of ourselves as a purposeful, growing species."

– Octavia Butler

Cosmos—source of life expressing itself in physical form. Vast, complex, impossible to fully imagine and quite possibly never ending.

To take pause and see with your mind's eye what is beyond the blue skies of day and the periphery of stars visible from our neighborhoods is to be more fully in connection with the truth of existence. Looking at photographs of our own galaxy and interstellar phenomenon, light years away, it is at once familiar (as a twinkling in my body) yet beyond human experience and uninhabitable in human form. We are left with our capacity to feel into the Cosmic realm in both its immensity and interconnectivity. Contemplating Cosmic measurements—a constellation 13 billion light years away—pushes us to expand our perceptual boundaries and allows space for new perspectives. Wondering about the whole of existence as an interwoven, expanding system of unfathomable dimensions is a worthwhile endeavor.

Before the emergence of the Cosmos, was there a void? Perhaps from the silence of nothing, the spark of life emerged as an impulse to give. *Giving form to another*...the source of life can be conceived as giving and receiving, the essence of love. The connection between individual entities infinitely manifesting can be felt as the eternal flow of unconditional love.

Exploring Cosmos with our hearts and minds, we can step into current scientific theories about the origins of life to find inspiration for collaboration and sharing resources for the betterment of all. To experience life from a Cosmic perspective is to find kin in the very first subatomic particles of existence. Our ancestors go beyond generations, descending from the very first microbes of life, quickening in each breath we take here and now.

To imagine dark matter and other Cosmic particles as loving intelligence, releases love from its entrapment as a singular human concept. Attachment is found at the edges of love between entities, moving broadly into awareness of interconnection between all things. Perhaps enlightenment is perception of self and other as beings of the same fabric of existence, weaving in and out of dimensional realities. This metaconsciousness can provide clarity with regard to the nature of Cosmos: broadening, as life energy; and flowing through itself. as love. The universal language of Cosmic wholeness can be found in the beating heart, shifting molecule, flutter of wings, and turning of the tide.

Cultivating a conscious relationship with the Cosmos is a wisdom practice that can be chosen to amplify one's embodied understanding of the interbeingness of all forms of life. Sit and listen to the Cosmos—by whatever name you call it, whatever tradition you find it, whatever freedom you need to experience it. Sitting in the heart, at the center of existence, by imagining who you were before you were born (as the Buddhist koan recommends) is a useful way to step out of the confines of the individual self and access the field of Cosmic interconnection.

Through its singular stars and mysterious unified dance, Cosmos teaches us to experience the non-dual: the simultaneous individual self and oneness of all things. Meditating with Cosmos inspires me to have hope for a peaceful softening of the harsh qualities of human evolution. The pain of competition for survival, wars over resources and territories, the development of weapons, oppression of peoples; each opens my heart to the night sky in hope for a path back to understanding the source of oneness. Conflicts echoing fear and destruction bring forth a desire for wholeness—the source of life driving us to find what we already have. Contemplation of Cosmic interconnection offers the opportunity, each moment, for a less brutal path, a more graceful way to smooth the cutting edges to minimize pain in growth.

Putting ourselves in perspective through starry awe, we are able to find peaceful paths of reciprocal collaboration, to catch moments of injustice as soon as they arrive, to balm with equity as we treat one another as flesh of the same reflected light.

From this stance, emergent challenges are brought to fullness; they become information to cultivate peace and mutual support through thriving integration so that injustice does not fester. We fill our hearts and minds with discernment of collective learning and breathe with Cosmic presence, humble. Filled by the greatness of which we are a part, we are provided with never-ending generosity to extend through loving wisdom, fierce moral guidance and courage to relinquish fear.

Contemplating Cosmos can elicit deep knowing within your body. This knowledge may be experienced as empathy, caring, curiosity, and soulful endeavor. Using our sensory imagination to resonate with Cosmic grace illuminates our unity and can also expand our awareness far beyond our bodies. One can encompass the globe in a field of knowing and breathe deeply, extending further out. From our inner sense of our own soul, we shift into the bigger picture, the broad scale of life, our natural affinity with creation. We begin to sense the longevity of linear time by the billions, backwards and forwards. We can then lift ourselves *out* of our sense of linear time and immerse ourselves in the eternal space of presence. The Cosmos speaks to us, becomes us. From this eternal flow, all things are possible; the radical imagination finds room to grow and resources to create.

A practice of direct experience in contemplation with the Cosmos allows us to touch the magnitude of space, and, subsequently, the possibility of multidimensionality. To feel closer to the mysteries of planets, stars, solar systems, and galaxies becomes familiar, even normal to us. Engaging life from the subatomic to the infinite, we locate ourselves in the broadness of existence. From this vantage point, immersed in diversity, mystery, and the love that ultimately allows us to embrace life, we begin naturally to be more gracious to one another.

ONE HEART JUSTICE

Perhaps you already live in an expanded state, or your consciousness sits in a sphere just right for your existence. When I attune with this greater realm as far as I can, I grow into a field of graceful intelligence. The Cosmos inspires me to shift from the micro (the trees) to the macro (the forest, and beyond) with the intention of creating a more balanced life on Earth for all beings. Once In this greater realm, we recognize ourselves in all of creation; each aspect of life is revered and kept well, as the lineage of one's own family, and given the opportunity to thrive within the complex cycles of life and death.

Some cultures have ignored the Cosmos altogether and created systems seemingly apart from it, yet, as all is intertwined, this approach, by denying the truth, damages the greater whole. Cosmos is an open system, modeling ways of paying attention and listening to all aspects of life. Cultures that have engaged in close relationships with the natural world through their ways of living, eating, and healing, as well as through art and mythology, from ancient to modern times, light the way for a global reconnection to the Cosmic whole for humanity. In our collective quest to reconnect with the natural world, we must understand it is neither through co-optation of nor passing responsibilities to cultures deeply interconnected with Cosmos through their relationships with nature that will allow us to reimagine our way to global solutions. We each have a choice to find within our own hearts a connection to the heart in all things. It takes courage to know ourselves as valuable beings of creation simply for being alive and to honor this truth, for all beings and in all things. The root of this universal wisdom, available within one's own humanity, can be cultivated for the greater good with respect and creativity. To integrate this reverent consciousness with the cutting edge of our most advanced understandings and technologies is to give pertinent, precious fuel to our drive for progress. This universal perspective can become distorted when taken too far from the source of heart-based connection. It is important to acknowledge the human tendency for hegemonic disconnection from the whole that has allowed us to deem ourselves as superior to nature and to people whose ways of being have been and are deeply intertwined to a core, sacred connection with the natural world and a Cosmic understanding of interdependence.

Once we have experienced our familial oneness with the Cosmos, it becomes quite clear that part of our collective responsibility as humans is to restore resources, protection, and power to all peoples and aspects of life. Contemplating Cosmos activates responsibility to practice a deep connection with the natural world and reconnect with the Cosmic pillar of human consciousness. We cannot remain disconnected from this awareness rooting us to our own planet and expect to progress. And in order to cultivate this more equitable and unified balance to the planet, a heart-based approach to transformation toward restoration and innovation is the most effective choice.

What would occur if humanity increasingly inspired one another to unite through the global value of interconnectivity from a heart-based perspective? We have reached a point in our evolution in which we have grown too far adrift in our human-made systems from the most enduring of human values and ecological foundations. All of humanity and all forms of life are vital to the conversation of how to move forward globally. Cosmos reminds us: no one culture, worldview, or way of life can be dominant. The practice of attuning to a Cosmic consciousness allows for unity in diversity, leading back to the very emergence of existence. Embodying interdependence allows for integration on all fronts of ingenuity: in science, technology, math, medicine, architecture, and allocation of resources. The practice of opening oneself to the vast experience of Cosmic existence and expansion brings one back to the deepest, most vital taproot of our species so that we may communicate with all species, honorably evolving as a whole, thriving network.

Every person, every animal, every plant, every element emerges from the source of life, creating a channel of love through which giving and receiving occurs. This fundamental Cosmic truth, experiencing the reciprocity of all of life, can help guide our current, errant systems, because we have forgotten our place of interconnection with each other and with the planet. Generally, humans have developed other aspects of our capacities and now require deep integration of our education, technology, transportation, science, medicine, and more, with our ecological and Cosmic realities. A Cosmic perspective allows for integration of our greatest advances with the understanding that we are a part of nature and not apart from nature. Otherwise, it will be humanity that joins other species who have already passed from existence due to this imbalance, as we follow our own path of demise. Choosing to prioritize the consciousness of interconnection through open inquiry is the radical pursuit of modeling human society on natural systems for the betterment—and continuance —of all of life.

Allowing the experience of Cosmos to guide us into systems of life that sustain us is not in opposition to progress. It is vital for humanity to keep our feet on the ground and our heart's open, and to inform our minds when it comes to the leading edge of each field of inquiry. It is vital to seek integration, in tandem with cooperative competition, within our own collective mind. For example, when science and technology are approached from the intention of bringing cohesion to the greater whole, of cultivating diversity—be it biological, neurological, or cultural—it creates a feedback loop in which the intention for all of creation to thrive informs the trajectory of advancement. To rebalance a global, collective evolution is to reallocate all resources, beginning with the resource of one's individual energy: physical energy, spiritual energy, and intellectual energy.

When I attune to the Cosmic field, I hear it reminding us that when we limit the consciousness, voice, growth, and contribution of our fellow humans with the constructs of oppression—both psychological and systematic—we limit the possibility for a more thriving world. Heart-based leadership, connected to the limitless power of Cosmic inspiration, increases devotion to the whole and provides guidance toward thriving integrative interaction, in policy, design, and outcome. We can take heart that systems led by fear and the clutching of power are feudal when compared to the eternal force of life, adaptation of spirit, and the will to actualize. To insist on limiting or monitoring another's connection, from a heart-based perspective, is to start down the road to fundamentalism and collective decline. When each person makes choices, moment by moment, to engage the world around them, present to the truth that we are more intricately interconnected than we can possibly conceive, it is clear that free will to connect to the Cosmos is essential.

In many endeavors it is wise to have expansive parameters of research to open our hearts and minds to the broad mystery and intricacy of the Cosmos. Each being finds its way, like an axiom finding its way through the neural network of the great mind of the universe. This is only a dangerous endeavor

ONE HEART JUSTICE

when we seek to enforce our own idea of what an individual life should be, as opposed to creating the most thriving environments for one another. A hopeful—and a practical—way forward is for each one of us to harness universal love, curiosity, compassion, and respect to move all aspects of human development outward from the center of a heart-based intelligence that is both sustainable and prolific.

To choose to connect to the Cosmos is to understand oneself as both a human animal fully immersed in the day and time of our finite lives and also an essential true self or soul infinitely connected to eternal wholeness. To locate one's existence in this field of presence is a way to bridge seeming paradoxes. This form of contemplation compels us toward a more cohesive whole, without succumbing to or relying on the brutality of illusive control and dominance. It takes courage to let go of the cravings of the false self and attune to a greater wisdom beyond our individual cares and wants. Yet, perhaps surprisingly, we do not have to abandon our comforts, our rituals, our desires, our very human nature to practice living from a broader place. When we practice caring about the other, our neighbor, being open to another's ritual, another's expression, another's comfort, we extend a generosity far beyond humanity, into the natural world, and all our needs are met.

It is the natural world that seeks to inform us, the natural world of which we are created, watching us, waiting for humanity collectively to reconnect to the lessons of wisdom, respect, and courage, through a broadened perspective. How do we make a *faster* collective shift to the design and implementation of systems that restore a thriving and sustainable world? In a living system, any attempt to mandate, police, coerce or manipulate a way of being, even with the best intentions, can lead to imbalance, distrust and divisiveness. A living system is an organic system that develops and is cultivated by choice and willingness. Through the will to endure, learn, inspire and be inspired this shift can be made, choice by choice, as the universal heart informs the mind.

Developing a relationship with all aspects of creation, with the Cosmos as a whole, ever-expanding entity of interconnection, is not in opposition to objective science. It encompasses science in its capacity to be as open and objective as possible when understanding the physical world. Where there is heart-based curiosity there is careful observation and motivation to use information for the best possible universal outcomes.

There is an unseen aspect to all of life that we experience in dreams, and there are other intangible aspects of spirit within the field of interaction that are happening between life forces, held and influenced by what we understand as the physics of the universe. It is possible to be aware of these aspects and to know that they can change at any moment. To celebrate the progress of science and to bask in the mysteries of Cosmos are mutually inclusive experiences that can illuminate a broader conversation.

As humans, we can experience ourselves full of the spirit of the Cosmos, the spirit of manifest life. It is important to acknowledge that equal to the drive to dominate and survive are adaptations to exist in symbiosis with one's environment—that it is with equal measure that human beings have endured through cooperation, empathy, collaboration, and respect for the environments in which they coexist. When moving toward the need to defend oneself, emotionally, intellectually and physically, one must consider the ramifications of aggression and differentiate that need with an assertion toward safe space to grow. Nonviolent approaches are longer lasting, and in turn more effective, when moving with the ebb and flow of dynamic systems of life. When we function within ourselves, our homes, our communities, our environments as one planet, we open our minds, our hearts, and our experiences in kinesthetic ways to the information of each individual's existence within our society and each element of the ecosystem. Our call is to listen and distill this information through compassionate leadership, to move the whole in directions mutually beneficial for all, with the Cosmos as our inspiration. There have been great contributions made by individuals, collectives, and institutions who seek this cause through religion, philosophy, art, and many other fields. By employing the currency of wonder, love, contemplation, nonviolent action, and diplomacy, through careful study we create innovative approaches as stewards for the fundamental elements of life sustained in equal measure.

We must not fall weary of being open to learning or being wrong, and be ready to adapt by staying open to channels of information and dynamic change. By embracing a daily commitment of attuning in mind, body, and spirit to something beyond us, a Cosmology of oneness develops beyond the beliefs and experiences of the past. To experience the force of life as a loving whole can allow one to fulfill a life of individual purpose and meaning, connected to the advancement of the greater whole. Each person engages in their own unique way and developmental path. As humans, we can be so misguided in how we value existence as to forget each human being is life itself, universes unto ourselves. To connect with the Cosmic core of every plant, animal, and aspect of life on the planet is to speak a language of true power.

Money is a common construct devised to exchange energy and value. Current global economic systems viewed from a

Cosmology based on the source of oneness, avert and distort our most vital resources. Unless and until our monetary systems and all resources are calibrated with the dynamic flow of Cosmic love—giving and receiving for the betterment of all—humanity will fall short in its quest to keep the planet turning, even for its own species.

How do we restore equal balance, reduce global warming to save ourselves, to save other species, to save our planet as we know it? What if the seeds of change are held in each breath and choice of the moment? If that sounds daunting, it is only because our minds immediately jump to the Other: how to convince the Other, how to change the mind of the Other, how to manipulate the resources of the Other so that our own system or policy prevails. As human beings, we have shown how brutal, shortsighted, selfish, and corrupt we can be. We have also demonstrated how giving, selfless, connected and innovative we are. What is the force we can share to evolve by applying our most altruistic innovations? What is it that we can each embody, of our own choosing, to prosper?

As I listen to the Cosmos, I hear it saying the human psyche is part of the invisible realm, formed through intricate connection, experience, memory, biology, neurons, hormones, environment, relationship, and more. To embrace complexity from deep resonance with existence is not to submit to ignorance. It is a choice to engage in integrating experience informing all aspects of life, study, creation, and development. To embrace the force of life as a loving ally, even in the face of one's individual mortality, is to embody the full power of life's potential and the power of human potential for growth into a holistic, altruistic creation.

Through kinesthetic awareness of Cosmic expansiveness we can write a narrative of human progress in which we play

ONE HEART JUSTICE

our necessary role in listening to the fundamental elements of life as equal entities in healing the planet. The notion that nature is watching us is the seed from which this consciousness grows. We are nature, watching ourselves begin to understand how our disconnection is leading many species to go extinct; alerting us to the need to make radical shifts within our environments. Who will come to save us from our own demise? It is possible the future lies in choices each one of us make, and that the most dire choice does not lie in finding the right ways to dispose of our trash but in how we perceive ourselves and the world around us. One possibility is to embrace the Cosmos as a living system we are part of, not in control of, not in battle with, but in a reciprocal learning process with. Engaging all beings equally creates space for ideas, dialogue, and methodology, connecting us to the roots of creation and possibility. To broaden the professionalization of postmodern society in order to consider a Cosmic perspective is not to devolve into nature worship. It is a way to engage our living world with ingenuity, personal freedom, and sound intellect.

Many wisdom traditions tell us that from deep misunderstanding and misalignment can emerge the light of understanding and resilience. Imagine humanity is collectively going through a dark night of its soul, in which the tyranny of fear and misplaced power, the tragedy of murdered lives and prolonged suffering of oppression threatens to condemn it to a traumatic trajectory. This drive toward global tragedy sets the stage for the Cosmos to retake our imaginations to envision a heart-based, intelligent, grounded, sacred connection with all of life. As we progress to a collective understanding, embracing the non-dual, we understand that to embrace imagination is not to deny logic and to follow the heart is not to dismiss current facts and knowledge. When all faculties of humanity are embraced in their fullness—within ourselves and one another—true equity begins to radiate outward with a force willing to take on the most atrocious missteps of our own creation.

What is it like to bring this moment-to-moment practice of listening to the Cosmos into our daily lives? Sitting outside, I connect to Cosmos from my heart and hear the cicadas, ever familiar and yet unseen. One of a multitude of life cycles reminding me there is an eternal song all of life is a part of, and I am open to the never-ending inquiry. I experience the Cosmos as space with no beginning or end, and as part of this force I become an aspect of the narrative of life unfolding. Being nourished by and making meaning through the spirit of Cosmos, I seek to understand and shape the world around me, through story. Creating an ever-evolving Cosmic story is a process through which the energy of life can be woven into awareness. When this kind of narrative is founded on the principles of love, collaboration, and reciprocal relationships, these values become central to the reality of life in all its forms. Integrating the language of love into our understanding of the Cosmos is a universal tool, effective for co-creation. This unifying energy can allow each one of us to cast off unhelpful beliefs and patterning to find freedom in our own unique capacities. The act of self-love is to experience oneself as a most worthy, valuable aspect of the source of all things. Many barriers fade when allowing universal beauty to permeate oneself in connection with the beauty in all of life.

Cosmic resonance can guide our way, through cultural dexterity into boundless ranges of interconnectivity. We are no longer held back by beliefs and structures that emerge solely from territorial logic. When we tap into the eternal system of existence, we naturally follow an evolutionary path that serves

ONE HEART JUSTICE

every aspect of humanity, the planet, and the abundance of species that work together to create life on earth.

Cosmos is the grand space of free will, the open field. We are invited instinctively to *play* and discover within it, being curious enough to allow it to speak to us, through us, and as us. Universal awareness brings the creative process into the present moment of every aspect of our lives. My whole body listens as I reconnect with the loving embrace of Cosmic existence. I am able to trust the bigger picture as one would trust a thriving guide of wisdom. Then, stress ensues, my expanded state of interconnection shrinks, I am focused on the urgent need at hand. The moment passes, I have responded, or overreacted to the situation. I feel separate from the greater process, the mysterious whole of creation in its flow. I take a moment to reconnect, and the presence of the Cosmos feels eternal, ever ready to be rejoined. I ask Cosmos, why reconnect, why not stay myopic in the details of my own singular existence? I hear Cosmos answer in the word "grace." The grace of putting my own life in the context of the greater whole, providing meaning, patience, acceptance and purpose. I sit in the sun for a moment in between tasks and wonder how I know Cosmos is speaking to me? Is it the limits of my own imagination answering back? It is both and more. Cosmos holds me at the edge of my understanding and invites me to open to broader complexity and nuanced presence. My mind wants to understand the stressful moments and aspects of life and how they fit in with the overall process of life. I understand that stress, and to a greater extent, crises, are moments of swift transformation. An opportunity to embrace what happens on the other side of challenge and continue toward a vision of life on Earth where all beings thrive. Cosmos does not reveal itself to be fully understood but offers moments of deep knowing and threads of information to those who pay attention with openness and passion. The mind can only begin to piece together the puzzle of the seemingly dichotomous and of paradox into a cohesive whole. It is the heart that is truly integrative when intending to inform each moment with love for all, including oneself—allowing us to rehumanize ourselves and others.

It is also important to create tough, loving barriers when embodied life around us is out of touch with the source that forms it and shifts out of interconnected mutual benefit. I create boundaries in order to be able to love more deeply, while simultaneously approaching the world with the intention of maintaining my own source connection, in order to connect fully to others. I am committed to looking deep within to witness and accept the blind and wounded parts of myself so that I may do the same when I see and am with others. What we know from our ancestral learnings is that there are unending benefits in our abilities to have compassion and empathy, and to strive for forgiveness in order to embrace the multitude of beautiful, tragic complexity in which each human being exists. To welcome these traits within ourselves and one another, the Cosmos points to traditions that help us to continue to understand how to use our emotions as information in the wisest ways, and teaches us to increase awareness of fear, anger, sadness, loneliness, and joy to fulfill the most beneficial aspects of the emotional, psychological, relational, and intellectual capacities of being human.

The practice of tuning in, through whole-body presence in meditative moments, to the notion of an ever-changing, expanding Cosmos has allowed me to have a visceral experience of what I can describe as a field of unconditional love, in which all dimensions of life interconnect on multiple levels.

ONE HEART JUSTICE

One way to consider these levels is the invisible or spiritual, the sub-particle or mostly invisible, and the physical—able to be knowingly touched. As the ups and downs of my personal life unfold on a daily basis, I take moments to understand what I can learn from feeling this illuminated field of love brought to me through the Cosmos. How can this field of unconditional love, the source of oneness, help me as a mother struggling with the development of her children? How can this golden field illuminate my personal gifts and help me to accept my shortcomings so that I can affect change toward a more equitable, safe, thriving community of life? I find that as I sit and listen, I hear the Cosmos echoing from its own source of oneness through the expanse of unending love, into what we understand as galaxies, space, and filtering all the way down into what I am experiencing as a human being in this particular day, time, body, age, and identity—and that all of these things are very real and yet quite temporary. I realize that I have been grasping to control various aspects of my life and the world around me, and this listening draws me to ask deeper questions about boundaries, control, influence, and inspiration. What are the differences between all of these impulses within me? How does that relate to being in a flow with the larger expression and inner workings of all of life?

First, I hear the Cosmos saying, *Let go. Let go of all the strings you are trying to pull, the foundations you are trying to build and the paths you are trying to create. Take a moment and let go; and once you let go, a kind of realignment can happen allowing fresh images, fresh goals, fresh ideas, and interventions to emerge.*

For me, the personal influence of Cosmic contemplation is to be present within a never- ending process...like the birth and death of a mollusk whose shell is tumbled about in the ocean and lands at my feet, becoming a symbolic gesture of what it once was and the dream of life living itself. When anger, sadness, hopelessness, and pain become the essential experience of my day-to-day life, listening to the Cosmic field reminds me that these feelings are not places of arrival, but intensive transformative processes. It feels as though my soul and spirit are connected to Cosmic oneness, just as my human heart is connected through vessels to provide the current of life for my physical body. The same pulse of life that causes the heart to beat helps me to feel joy, generosity, curiosity, and peace, to give and receive. My heart, filled with universal, Cosmic energy is enlivened with nourishment, compassion, kindness, acceptance, gratitude, and moreover, is the flow of awareness connecting all of creation to the source of one unifying whole.

I hear the Cosmos calling us to cultivate each being's natural gifts to sew the fabric of a loving whole. Collectively we can broaden our consciousness by nourishing one another into fullness of presence so vast we can barely fathom the beauty.

ONE HEART JUSTICE PROCESS
Universal Heart Meditation

Visit Oneheartjustice.com for guided meditation recording of One Heart Justice process

To begin the Universal Heart Meditation, bring your whole body into awareness and allow whatever needs to dissolve into the void of nothingness to release and fade away. Breathe into this dissolution state and relax into stillness. When you are ready, allow the source of life to emerge through your heart center and breathe deeply into your heart. As you exhale, know that you are in connection with the one source of all creation. Feel your heart spark with the intelligent life force causing it to beat. Allow the spark of life's source to alight in each of your energy centers moving up to your throat center, your third eye center, crown center and up above your head rooting into the source of life. Bring your awareness back down through each energy center and feel the spark of source life energy to blossom in your solar plexus center, your belly center, root center and down into your feet and below rooting into the source of life. Remember you are created of this one magnificent source, illuminating your heart, all of you, and all the innumerable manifestations of creation on Earth and beyond.

From your radiant heart center, and all of your energy centers you can envision and feel this loving source intelligence radiating out from your body, until you are fully residing in a sphere of unconditional love. Stay here for a moment and soak in love as if you are a plant soaking in light.

As you experience the awareness of your whole body within the sphere of universal love, you can allow this energy to continue to expand in all directions, radiating further and further, as far as your sensory awareness and imagination will expand, until you know that you have expanded fully. Feel the love of the universe coming back toward you, enveloping your expansion in a hug, and know that you are fully interconnected with the web of life. From this place, born of the source of all of creation and connected through the force of love, you can begin to listen, ask for guidance, share and receive information.

Hold the spirit of Cosmos in your heart, your mind, and your body. Be present with whatever arises. As always, if this feels uncomfortable, you may try shifting from fear to curiosity. If you begin to feel overwhelmed in any way, take a break from the practice and engage in self soothing and getting support. When contemplating Cosmos feels right, continue into Somatic Listening.

Somatic Listening

As you move into Somatic Listening and listen with your whole body by being nonjudgmentally aware of body sensations, images, words, cognitive impressions, and emotional tones, imagine these are ideas allowing you to learn with Cosmos. If you lose focus, bring your awareness back to you heart center and smile, feeling the presence of Cosmos in your heart as you breathe and regain focus. Notice what sensations, images, emotions, and words draw your attention most and feel powerful to explore further. Ask Cosmos what messages it has for you to deepen your understanding of leading through interbeing. Allow the spirit of Cosmos to illuminate your throat energy center or any other energy center that feels right. As you hone in on impressions to transition into creative exploration with, take a moment to make notes or draw in your journal, or amplify body sensation into movement, or sound. Use whatever ways seem most effective to bring expression and understanding to your Somatic Experience with Cosmos that is the right way for you today.

Creative Exploration

As you move into the third aspect of the creative contemplation process, Creative Exploration, know that you can return to the Universal Heart Meditation and Somatic Listening at any time, and then back into Creative Exploration.

Your expressive arts practice can be in any artistic medium. You may choose to take your sensory experience into movement, visual arts, sound, or music. You can also focus on a problem you are solving, a current project, a relationship you are in process with and ask Cosmos to support you with new approaches and ideas. The wisdom you gain in contemplation with Cosmos is yours to create with in whatever way that is best for you.

Make this experience your own as you move in and out of Universal Heart Meditation, Somatic Listening, and Creative Exploration at your own pace. Be authentic to your own practice and allow your own patterns and methods to emerge. Begin to notice in every day life how the Cosmos is present and how you can sense it as an intelligent force that is familiar in it's connection to your mind, body, and soul

CHAPTER THREE

Earth – Connect Through Healing Resonance

"Is a black shambling bear, ruffling its wild back and tossing mountains into the sea"

- *Lucille Clifton*

The source of life celebrates, with deep reverence, the diverse confluence of Earth's beauty. Abounding with subatomic particles in various combinations, Earth is the great variety of interconnected life from invisible molecules to soaring mountains. Intelligent, with resilient adaptivity, Earth teems with

ONE HEART JUSTICE

evolutionary energy, creating the milieu for intricate intertwining and flowing with phenomenological creativity.

Feeling Earth as a conscious entity, whole and full, holding my life's presence, I accept that my body is inextricably connected to the planet. I am part of Earth; my body belongs nowhere else. In meditation, I catch a glimpse into the span of the billions of years that Earth has evolved and the millions of years in which hominids have come and gone. We have both adapted to and disrupted Earth's biomes.

In contemplation with Earth, I hear it say it will continue on as a planet even if humans change the environment to the point of a drastically altered reality or of non-existence for ourselves. Earth says it is time for human evolution to fully reintegrate our awareness with the wisdom of the nature we are—through the potential of our heart centers. We are at once singular physical beings as well as beings made of and for Earth. Earth marvels at our discoveries, the complexities of our minds and variations of our bodies. It witnesses us trying to evolve by creating things outside of ourselves and asks us to turn inward and experience our bodies in deep connection with Itself…to contemplate in meditative states the ways in which Earth itself can support us in developing the characteristics we need to collaborate toward a shift in planetary direction.

Cultivating our capacity to forgive, take accountability, establish and sustain trust, as well as to listen deeply to each other and nature, is essential for humanity to progress. Each person is unique in the way their body, mind, and soul intersect and inform each other; so each person's growth and contribution when engaging with these concepts will be right for them.

In an effort to strengthen my relationships and practice heart-based interpersonal connection, Earth guides me to contemplate the hurt that I am carrying from others, in this lifetime and beyond, as well as the pain I have caused others. Earth helps me to see these unhealed experiences in my physical and energy bodies as knots in a greater energy field that I can choose to focus on healing and clearing in order to be a more open channel for the regenerative flow Earth offers.

Earth brings my awareness to my heart center and wants me to connect with Its center—its heart and soul, its singular intelligent beingness as a creation of the source of life. Earth says *let me nourish you*, so I hold all the pain I've caused and experienced in my body and energetic field in my awareness, and feel energy coming from the center of Earth and up through my body. It gently begins to resolve emotional pain from the past that is stored in my body, and increases my cohesive presence. I appreciate Earth's support in healing, and know I can return to this forgiveness meditation anytime.

I feel Earth requesting more humans to connect our hearts with it's center—the heart of Earth; to envision this connection and embody this resonance. We can imagine our heartbeats synchronizing so we are in sync with the whole of Earth. We can feel the circulatory system of Earth's waters flowing with the water of our own bodies, moving in precise unity with vital calming nourishment. In this resonant state with Earth, we can encounter new ways of being, communicating, and creating. We can engage in meditative somatic practices to harness a path forward for humanity's collaboration with Earth. We each have the choice, the opportunity, to join with Earth in alignment toward a more balanced ecological and psychological whole. There are many ways to do this, including contemplative practices to increase embodied psychological and spiritual knowing. This form of awareness and presence can support us in *becoming* the body of knowledge we seek to find.

Earth has much to teach about resonance. From the perspective I am sharing with Earth in meditation, *resonance* is the practice of attuning, with another being or aspect of life with healing intentionality toward a more harmonic, vibrant, interconnective whole. Earth brings this potential to my understanding, because it will be mutually beneficial when humans collectively believe that meta-awareness and deep reverence and sensitivity with our planet can be transformative. Engaging in Earth-based meditations will help us to understand ourselves and Earth in ways that have yet to be discovered, or are ready to be rediscovered. The concept of resonance pushes the boundaries of what many understand as the function of meditation and enlivens us to the possibility that interconnectivity goes beyond a sense of greater peace and deeper meaning, but it is in fact a scientific principle discovering itself through humanity's efforts.

Earth reaches out to humanity through the meditative field with an offer to support us in coevolution. It asks us to begin to trust it as a guiding presence. Earth shares that it can strengthen our trust in ourselves and one another. The teaching Earth has about trust is to practice attuning our whole selves to the truth of the moment. Making this part of a meditative practice can help us to let go of illusions, false selves, as well as concepts and relationships that are not beneficial for us. Facing a falsehood ultimately can only propel us into deeper knowing of truth, but if we struggle against entering the field of truth, not facing a falsehood can generate a process of prolonged struggle. Falsehoods cause unnecessary pain and distraction from the celebration of the one truth of loving wholeness. Yet falsehoods can never detract from or destroy the truth of oneness.

While humanity may collectively continue repeating patterns of competition, toward our own demise, it is the better part of ourselves that will witness our transformation, one way or another, through the awareness of true interconnection.

The choice to trust always comes with the risk of betrayal, and Earth offers humanity strength, in the courage of discernment, to form alliances of heart-centered individuals to shift structures necessary for healthy change. Earth reminds us: our fears can be soothed by Earth itself to help us develop collaborative communities so that we may thrive as a species. Earth acknowledges the pain and suffering humanity experiences due to other aspects of the natural world. We are harmed by weather, disease, and other animals. Earth invites us to open our hearts and minds to the perspective of working together—with each other and the natural world—in a context of mutual respect. Engaging through integrative respect, as opposed to fear-based dominance, allows us to progress, just as our ability to share with one another has always been the reason homo sapiens have endured. Adapting to changing climates and other forms of life that harm us and cause us disease, has been the very pressure of adversity that helped develop our prefrontal cortex—a primary catalyst of human evolution. Earth calls us now to develop our meta-awareness as an evolving species to further integrate our hearts and minds. As we come closer to fully understanding the benefits of a cohesive brain-state, we illuminate the need for a unified, heart-centered, body-mind state, in connection with our planet and the universal source of life.

Earth clearly offers, to those willing to listen, guidance toward the next chapter of human evolution being heart-based meta-awareness. In order to step off of the wheel of progression and regression as evidenced by continued wars, cycles of autocracy, and global economic practices rapidly damaging nature, we will individually need to continue choosing and practicing loving ourselves and one another. Earth asks us to understand love on a deeper level by connecting with it's presence through various meditative states. It reminds us we will need more than policies and technologies to move into a more balanced way of life. The level of intricate, diverse intelligence propagating our planet calls us to reconnect, deepen, and cultivate our human nature. Feeling, caring, transforming, supporting, developing bonds is the forte of the human heart. *The human heart is the technology we have been looking for.* It is the untapped potential of the human heart that answers the call of reversing climate change and the unnecessary systems that have led us astray.

When in a meditative state with Earth, I am shown the power of the heart center. The heart center is like the control center for activating the underdeveloped qualities of humanity. Becoming aware of the source of life as the fuel that powers the heart center, ignites our ability to use the energy or electromagnetic force of the heart to enliven our other energy centers with loving intelligence and creates a sphere of lovingkindness. We ground ourselves by envisioning and embodying source energy to flow up and down our central channel. We can feel it flow down through the top of our heads, through our feet and into the center or heart of Earth. We allow Earth to send restorative and innovative energetic information up, through our central channel and into our heart centers and we blossom into a sphere of love. When we meditate in this way, body, mind, and spirit know we are integrating this healing energy into our everyday lives. Understanding this will inform us in the best ways.

As I sit with Earth in a meditative state this morning, I feel it answer the questions I hold after a particularly hard day of little conflicts yesterday with family. Earth reassures me: this practice of cultivating heart-based reconnection with ourselves and nature is not a perfectionistic endeavor. It calls for patience and appreciation of each being's individual consciousness, as well as our own. To engage in practices such as these is to increase love and deepen embodiment of interconnectivity. It is not to judge oneself or others, or coerce another into being more heart-focused. I connect my heart center with the core of Earth and ask it to inform my actions today in support of greater love for all to heal the planet.

Resonating my body with Earth I feel it encouraging humanity to listen to and honor our bodies and allow for a diversity of ways to nourish ourselves and our ecosystems, including eating plants, well-cared-for animals, and animal products that are most beneficial for each of us. Earth reminds me the food chain or predatory aspect of life is part of the Earth experience and that we can find balance in these relationships by not overreacting to animal threats to humanity, as well as by not over-killing other animals. We can interrelate and live more cohesively by finding ways to protect ourselves *and* subsist without damaging other living systems. Giving space for all aspects of life requires mutual respect and finding thoughtful responses to our own needs and those of other animals and life forms.

Wake up, Earth calls, as my body is enlivened by better eating and more exercise. *Wake up*—to our beauty, diversity and potential as we coevolve. Understand the protection necessary for healthy water, air, and plant and animal ecosystems. Feel the true wealth of the biodiversity that has been lost. Imagine a future in which new species emerge within

ONE HEART JUSTICE

protected habitats, just as new aspects of humanity develop from the best of what we can become.

I sit with the immensely complex systems that comprise all aspects of Earth. I think of myself and my family as complex systems on this planet. I understand that our challenges to function well together as individuals, from our most intimate relationships to our broadest organizations, have great bearing on long-term prospects. I wonder about emotional pain in my relationships as a parent, a partner, a child and sibling. I see how we are all so different in our needs and development. I am drawn again to practice letting go—to forgive, with the support of Earth energy flowing through me. I receive insight about connecting with others as opposed to trying to control or change others. I sit in presence with my fear of the unknown in my personal life and on a more global scale. I feel tender, vulnerable, and afraid for my children—our children. I remember the importance of sitting with the truth of life taking another life, and the physical and emotional pain of radical change—death. I hear Earth saying it will not become the vision of my dreams for more unity among humanity without hard change. *Earth, how do we get through the hard moments, and why are we here upon you and with you?* Earth's guidance to me is to live in the space between present-moment reality and embodied vision. To hold both experiences through integration created in partnership with Earth.

This week, I have been shaken out of my grounded state of embodied love, in a large way, by the accumulation of difficult experiences. Daily I stumble, but this week I am lost. Earth brings me strong grounding in my feet, for my purpose. Earth reminds me my purpose is to give myself enough care, to stay as fully present to life, to the truth of the moment, as I am able; to enliven my body daily with the source of life, to practice increasing my awareness and attunement with the universal elements, and to offer this practice to others.

Embodied vision is a concept Earth provides guidance for; it is consciousness energy, informing matter. I meditate with Earth and learn that embodied vision is knowing oneself as the source of all of life—knowing the fullness of sacred intelligence that is at once all of life *and* your individual body, mind, spirit presence. To sit with embodied vision is to understand that cultivating this source-energy presence is a graceful healing practice of acceptance, sacred celebration, and love. The vision aspect is experienced as each being knowing itself and others as the source of life. It engages in a unified field of consciousness that is powerful enough to harness the spirit of our planet. What I'm saying is: if we practice embodied vision, Earth could reach a level of consciousness that allows us to engage with other dimensions, solar systems and life forms that have reached this point of evolution or beyond.

I practice being in the truth of each moment and embodying universal source energy. I feel Earth saying there are many people wanting to have experiences of unified consciousness through deep states of loving interconnection. Such group practices can be found throughout spiritual and contemplative communities with many different cultural, religious, and/or theoretical underpinnings. Earth affirms that meta-conscious connection with one another and with Earth itself, generates a field of inner and inter-knowing in which each diverse individual contributes to a greater force of synergetic cohesion. In this state, we are at once more ourselves and more than ourselves. It is a very satisfying experience for many and at the heart of coevolutionary opportunities. Earth reminds us to orient to the universal interconnection of life,

ONE HEART JUSTICE

in our relationships and in our concepts, to create in the most mutually beneficial ways.

Staying connected and reconnecting to the intergalactic grace of multidimensional eternity brings us each into our own sphere of being fully awakened as a soul in a human body. As a soul we know we are eternal, and as a body we know we are not. Holding this truth in experience helps us develop an organizing principle for oneness that makes sense to us, it will help us create unity in diversity.

To develop a principle of oneness is to believe that all of life is created of the same source and exists within a unified field of sacred presence. This state of being has been greatly lost in modern society, yet many people continue to practice ways of living within this awareness. Cultivating this embodied experience grounds us in ways that increase deep, authentic connection, a sense of peace, and loving expression.

I wonder if science will discover that when we intentionally enter alpha-theta brain states in connection with our heart centers, a pulse radiates through our energy centers and bodies, through our souls and connects our unified consciousness within the neural fabric of eternity unfolding. There are infinite ways to enter into a state of oneness; the only commonality is the human heart.

Earth guides me to feel the source of life spark within my heart center. To allow this spark to radiate as life energy up and down my central channel, opening my chakras and rooting my energy field above and below my body with the source of all that is. I bring my awareness back to my heart center and allow it to blossom like a sphere, moving through my body and intertwining with what feels like the neural fabric of source embodying my true integration with all that is. I feel all of myself—including my body—transform into particles, merging back into what I envision as the dark ground of being, like space itself.

Earth calls humanity to root ourselves in unconditional love. The kind of love that is stronger than individual beliefs, personal limitations, and traumatic wounding. Love that is grounded in: *I am human, you are human and we value each other's lives.* This sensibility extends to all of life on our planet and beyond. Earth calls us to study love, rooted in the source of all things.

Sharing universal love attuned with Earth broadens our hearts, and we overflow with appreciation and gratitude. Earth asks us to hold this presence as often as possible for as long as we can, to support others in feeling this experience. When we are upset, overwhelmed, tired and sick, practicing heart-based attunement with Earth brings a sense of peace, nourishment, rejuvenation, and healing strength.

This morning I wake up filled with doubt, separated from universal love in connection with Earth, due to big fears and little worries. I can't even name them all. I think of the food chain; how life subsists off of other life. I wonder where the line is between necessary violence and interconnected survival. I wonder about spiritual bypass, identity, privilege, and oppression. Where does universal love reside when finding societal balance, equality, and equity? I feel into Earth for guidance and realize I am only catching glimpses of the power of love and the immensity of life. Earth in its magnificent diversity and simultaneous wholeness as one organism teaches me that love is the opposite of fundamentalism. In answer to my questions about how to achieve equity, right action with all aspects of life on Earth—all peoples, all animals, plants, water, air—I understand there is no one way. In their most organic forms, equity, respect, safety, compromise, and humility are all facets of love

ONE HEART JUSTICE

necessary to cultivate right action, moment to moment, being to being. This recognition does not preclude the rule of law, and looks toward the enforcement of our own well-developed cultural integrity to support us to abide by the power of love within all else. Earth calls on humanity to evolve through our fears: to understand that fear of one another, fear of discomfort and death, fear of ourselves drives many of our cycles of tragedy and trauma. Earth asks us to own our fears, to harness and embrace them, and to understand how they relate to love. Our fears can be transformed through the truth they hold, which is that we value life.

Practicing heart-based understanding, we deepen our engagement in shared humanity. It is through sharing that we have survived and flourished. Earth guides us to remember to see ourselves in each other, to feel how we are alike, and to embrace our differences. May we extend this care and respect to the Earth itself. The human heart is generous. Earth reminds us to connect our hearts to our planet to benefit from the unending generosity of its abundance. We get confused when other forms of life harm us and believe we must fight back, eradicate, control. Earth says this perpetual overreaction is unnecessary and causes more harm than benefit. *Look for mutually inclusive solutions, seek to understand what other forms of life are moving toward. Find graceful ways to establish trust and guide one another toward minimal pain. Relish the beauty of the natural world, develop through it and around it. Shift economic structures that run counter to the flow of health and longevity. Restore dignity between all peoples.* Earth says this is what is possible: releasing fears and restoring love, moment to moment, with an open heart.

Earth as our living home offers us a chance to contemplate deep time as a way to transform our fears into valuing each moment for what it brings— to understand how fleeting our individual lives are within the context of Earth's life span and to find gratitude for one another's existence, here and now. What do we choose to learn, to share, to expand with our awareness? Earth as the birthplace of humanity is offering us opportunities for discoveries that will greatly enhance our experiences and bring more unity to our planet. We are exploring many of these areas now in fields of technological advancement, healing modalities, plant cultivation, restoring and protecting habitats. Yet Earth emphasizes we are collectively missing the key component that opens up unseen trajectories of understanding and creation: to listen to Earth itself—to cultivate our heart-based capacity to hear our own sacred planet in the way it shares information. Earth does not order us around, it does not shout, it offers each life form free will to adapt, to connect, to discover. And, if you learn to listen, it offers guidance, wisdom, and foresight toward creative adaptation and fullness of life.

Earth is not looking for prophets to proclaim its wants or its guidance. It offers each of us our own way of connecting, and my hope is that by sharing my experience with Earth in meditation I will help support you in your own way of connecting. Earth opens its heart to us, offering to connect to each person on their own terms, in sacred reverence for shared life. It is a subtle and gentle connection that can never be commodified or controlled, which is why it has all but disappeared from our daily practices in mainstream modern life. The art of listening to Earth has come and gone over the ages and lives on in land-based cultures in current time, and in those who are drawn to this aspect of their ancestral roots. Earth emphasizes the healing and transformative power of simply choosing to

ONE HEART JUSTICE

acknowledge It as a living being, and to hold it in our awareness in order to sense its presence. Earth says this is enough to revolutionize our understanding of human purpose. If in this process we become upset by what has already been destroyed of Earth and feel complicit and powerless, Earth guides us to continue to be fully present with that, just as we would a loved one going through changes or pain, or a loss we cannot change. Earth asks us to be steadfast in our love for it and to stay rooted in this connection. Earth asks us to understand that the genocide and degradation of indigenous cultures and peoples, people dismissed as "witches," and the relegation of Earth-based spirituality as New Age, magical thinking are ways dominant cultures have attempted to destroy and continue to devalue our ability to connect with Earth in creative and spiritual ways for the betterment of all. We can engage in Earth-based ways of knowing and continue to be modern, well-adjusted, intellectually adept people. We can integrate our awareness of Earth as a living being into our daily lives, our fields of study, our relationships and the ways we care for ourselves and others.

Meditating on Earth, and ourselves as emerging from the source of all things, is transformative in the ways we experience our own bodies and the bodies of others. As I increase my awareness and value of Earth as a living being, I increase my own body awareness, acceptance, and self-love. We are complex living organisms, changing each day—getting sick, getting well, having long term illness, dying. Earth asks us to hold our bodies in an awareness of what is working well, how we are thriving and adapting within limitation and pain as much as we are able, while holding us in our loss, anger, grief, and illness. Earth offers us resonance with its body—to feel the strength of life force within our own body and to appreciate its strength and beauty, in whatever state it is in. Attuning with Earth and its magnificent diversity supports our ability to let go of false criticism and contemporary standards of beauty, wellness, and ableism.

Appreciating Earth's variation supports us in expanding our perception of ourselves and others, to be body positive, and approach our own health and abilities with openness. I ask Earth why there have to be viruses, bacteria, genetic and cellular variations that harm and kill us? Earth reflects to me it is intentionally a place of adversity, designed to require evolution toward interdependence. The many forms of life on Earth can be perceived as competing for life and threatening one another's existence. Earth has compassion for the challenges, loss, and pain humans and other forms of life experience and understands that while it inspires wonder and pleasure, Earth is a hard place to be interwoven within. Earth asks humans to remember how much discovery and innovation have emerged from caring for one another in the face of its adversity, including fields of medicine, science, education, psychology, architecture, and more. Earth asks humanity to embrace a path forward that maximizes our capacity to care for one another indiscriminately and to be inclusive of caring for all other life forms as well. Equity and equality, recognized through heart-based practices, are essential to increase awareness of bias and prejudice within ourselves and in systems that keep us from caring for every person with the same generosity, respect, and methods that allow for quality of life and support for thriving growth.

Earth emphasizes that the ability to shift the practices that are causing global warming starts with each of us developing the qualities available within the human heart and extending these qualities toward one another. As we continue to learn

ONE HEART JUSTICE

to embrace one another equally and share resources so that each person thrives, we will be able to extend this right action to other animals, to plants, to air, to Earth itself. Earth loves all forms of life that have emerged, perished, and transformed within its realm. Earth reminds us that valuing other animals, plants, landscapes, elements, subatomic particles, and more will help us prioritize cultivating healthy ecosystems. Healthy systems generate cycles of health and will decrease sickness, disease, imbalance, and unnecessary violence.

As we visualize our whole bodies, held in source love emerging from our hearts, we will develop clarity about what is most nourishing to ourselves and the life we are surrounded by. Nourishing ourselves gives us the energy to nourish others, the land, air, plants, and water. How we treat ourselves and other people directly corresponds to how we treat the Earth. Our emotional, psychological, and spiritual wellness and growth require us to honor our planet with gratitude and care. Denial of this truth can leave us ungrounded as well as conceptually lost. Earth shows me that shining the light of love through our inner landscapes—be they physical, emotional, or spiritual—supports us in having a more peaceful, loving state of being. We can also shine this light of love within Earth itself as we align our heart centers with the center or heart of Earth in meditative visualization and connect with the peaceful and harmonious inner state of Earth's magnificent body.

Earth asks us to contemplate its levels of existence as similar to our own, as in: having a physical body, emotional/intellectual body, and soul/spirit body. These systems of experience integrate to create individual consciousness, in connection with universal consciousness. Earth shares its consciousness with me, and I am able to sense a bit of what it is like. Layers of landforms and temperatures in rotation, held in space by mass and gravity. Earth experiences itself as one being and as part of the Cosmic body. It connects with interstellar life in multiple dimensions, exchanging information through conductive fields like the underground, mycorrhizal networks of forests. Earth would like humans to keep practicing the experience of oneness. This will allow us to integrate our ways of life with all the other species on our planet, so that we suffer less and thrive within expanded connectivity.

Earth presents the neural networks of our bodies as an example of complex and beautifully integrated systems. It points to the heart center and other energy centers as openings to spiritual awareness, allowing meditative experiences that provide us with access and information far beyond our current technology. Earth seeks support through our cultivation of these resources, that we might interweave them with nature, metaphysically and technologically, using heart-focused intention. Sensing into our lifetimes, before and after our current human embodiment, allows us to live from our eternal presence and can empower us to focus our efforts on deep time sustainability.

Earth reminds us our souls exist, both before and beyond our current lifetime(s) on Earth. We exist beyond our bodies, as singular soul entities—part of the spirit of all that is. Earth wants us to know we are drawn to lifetimes here to experience the human body and connect with each other, plants, other animals, water, and the many opportunities Earth offers. Earth shares love and hope for humanity, and the intended focus we each arrive here with. The adversity of life on Earth can cause us to function primarily from fear. We are called to return to love as our primary orientation, as each of us is able. Love is interwoven with the fabric of existence, the source of all that

ONE HEART JUSTICE

connects us, and allows us to remember where we came from, what our purpose is, and where we return.

Earth can be a gentle guide and support in understanding our purpose on the planet. It is challenging to stay focused on our soul's purpose among all of the distractions we have created for ourselves. Yet it can be easy to rediscover, by listening to our deeper understanding. Some call it "soul searching"—the process by which you listen and feel deeply into your authentic calling. Our thoughts and beliefs can talk us out of our intuitive knowledge. Earth encourages us to identify our primary goal as human beings and to embody this in our daily process of accepting our limitations accepting the creative generativity of vision and limits.

Earth reminds us of our gift for creativity. Creativity is the process in which we embrace the present moment and coalesce what we know with what we are experiencing. We connect disparate concepts, materials, sounds, and actions to express, innovate, examine, and explore. Earth, as our foundation, underscores human creativity as far-reaching and endless. We are a species of thinkers and makers, working to survive and always creating change. Within this process are periods of struggle and doubt, inspiration and breakthroughs. Our creative guide, Earth asks us to believe in ourselves and be curious about our daily discoveries. To find hope in small successes and practice embodying our vision and purpose, even in times of great pessimism and setbacks. Earth reminds me of our ancestors, who kept vision for a better world and the resilience of the human spirit moving toward what is possible with heart-based collaboration, fueled by universal life, energy, and love.

I ask Earth about my anger and rage at injustice and oppression (that I am both an unwitting perpetrator and a victim of), and at the intentional and careless harm of other animals and living creatures. Earth affirms rage in response to injustice, control, and abuse, and encourages those focused on equitable change to be loud—to speak up with fierce intelligence, creativity, and passion. Working together and learning together, we can channel our anger with the force of collective, courageous focus. Earth emphasizes that rage can be transformed into nonviolent power, to shift consciousness. I ask Earth why it encourages nonviolent human processes when it forms earthquakes, volcanos, and many other violent aspects of creation that harm humans and other creatures. Earth answers that now I am beginning to understand *humanity's* higher purpose as a species on the planet. We are able to imagine a planet of increased awareness and capacity for collaboration to increase harmony for all of life. Earth reminds me: we have modern weather tracking technology, engineering and architecture, as well as indigenous practices of forest management and other Earth-caring methods. It asks us to further imagine integrating technology and ancient stewardship practices, with the intention of caring for Earth and all of life, as opposed to just protecting ourselves. We humans have great opportunities to collaborate and share, interculturally and globally, to restore and develop our planet in ways that may seem only like science fiction now—as is true for all progress. Earth lets me know it will always hold aspects of adversity, tragedy, and suffering, because that is an important thread of evolution and interconnection on this planet. Humans have the potential to greatly minimize these experiences and enhance loving interconnectivity and prosperity.

Earth asks me to explore evil, and I am guided in meditation to understand evil as a thought form completely disconnected

ONE HEART JUSTICE

from all that is. It exists throughout the universe, moving in reverse of the flow of love. The source of life created evil to be able to discover itself, eternally. The universe expands through opposites, in order to evolve through the process of discovery. Love needs evil, only to know itself as its opposite. This is why love will always overcome evil, why gratitude is more powerful than despair, and why faith is the most enduring fuel. Source allows us to shift evil simply by recognizing it as part of all that is; as an opportunity to join all things together through unconditional love, the ultimate healing power.

The universe is a welcoming place, all are welcome to remember where they are from and their place within the whole. Evil is redemptive within the field of all things. It gives us the opportunity to be reminded of our truth. Earth reminds us that evil is transformed by facing our fear of losing the essential parts of ourselves: When we live each day from a place of understanding that the most essential parts of ourselves are our souls and can never be destroyed, we are able to transform evil and ignorance within ourselves and our communities.

As the birds sing, here in the sun on this warm afternoon, I feel many radiant beings of light are present. It is as if each bird call resonates with interdimensional wisdom, beyond physical needs, echoing through layers of the unseen presence of life in many forms. I feel Earth supported by these mysterious beings of light, available through meditative states to provide guidance on how to be in connection with Earth to cocreate thriving evolution. There are Earth-like planets on an intergalactic scale, beyond our comprehension. These planets are in different phases of evolution. Some have evolved far beyond Earth, in terms of harnessing the power of unifying loving systems and radiating this harmonious potential throughout space-time. Listening to Earth, I feel it saying it has the potential to coevolve with humanity, to this way of being…if we choose to increase care and collaboration, and to cultivate our ability to exist within oneness consciousness.

ONE HEART JUSTICE PROCESS
Universal Heart Meditation

Visit Oneheartjustice.com for guided meditation recording of One Heart Justice process

To begin the Universal Heart Meditation, bring your whole body into awareness and allow whatever needs to dissolve into the void of nothingness to release and fade away. Breathe into this dissolution state and relax into stillness. When you are ready, allow the source of life to emerge through your heart center and breathe deeply into your heart. As you exhale, know that you are in connection with the one source of all creation. Feel your heart spark with the intelligent life force causing it to beat. Allow the spark of life's source to alight in each of your energy centers moving up to your throat center, your third eye center, crown center and up above your head rooting into the source of life. Bring your awareness back down through each energy center and feel the spark of source life energy to blossom in your solar plexus center, your belly center, root center and down into your feet and below rooting into the source of life. Remember you are created of this one magnificent source, illuminating your heart, all of you, and all the innumerable manifestations of creation on Earth and beyond.

From your radiant heart center, and all of your energy centers you can envision and feel this loving source intelligence radiating out from your body, until you are fully residing in a sphere of unconditional love. Stay here for a moment and soak in love as if you are a plant soaking in light.

As you experience the awareness of your whole body within the sphere of universal love, you can allow this energy to continue to expand in all directions, radiating further and further, as far as your sensory awareness and imagination will expand, until you know that you have expanded fully. Feel the love of the universe coming back toward you, enveloping your expansion in a hug, and know that you are fully interconnected with the web of life. From this place, born of the source of all of creation and connected through the force of love, you can begin to listen, ask for guidance, share and receive information.

Hold the spirit of Earth in your heart, your mind, and your body. Be present with whatever arises. As always, if this feels uncomfortable, you may try shifting from fear to curiosity. If you begin to feel overwhelmed in any way, take a break from the practice and engage in self soothing and getting support. When contemplating Earth feels right, continue into Somatic Listening.

Somatic Listening

As you move into Somatic Listening and listen with your whole body by being nonjudgmentally aware of body sensations, images, words, cognitive impressions, and emotional tones, imagine these are ideas allowing you to learn with Earth. If you lose focus, bring your awareness back to you heart center and smile, feeling the presence of Earth in your heart as you breathe and regain focus. Notice what sensations, images, emotions, and words draw your attention most and feel powerful to explore further. Ask Earth what messages it has for you to deepen your understanding of resonating through healing connection. Bring the spirit of Earth into your third eye center for insight and visions or any other energy center that feels right. As you hone in on impressions to transition into creative exploration with, take a moment to make notes or draw in your journal, or amplify body sensation into movement, or sound. Use whatever ways seem most effective to bring expression and understanding to your Somatic Experience with Earth that is the right way for you today.

Creative Exploration

As you move into the third aspect of the creative contemplation process, Creative Exploration, know that you can return to the Universal Heart Meditation and Somatic Listening at any time, and then back into Creative Exploration.

Your expressive arts practice can be in any artistic medium. You may choose to take your sensory experience into movement, visual arts, sound, or music. You can also focus on a problem you are solving, a current project, a relationship you are in process with and ask Earth to support you with new approaches and ideas. The wisdom you gain in contemplation with Earth is yours to create with in whatever way that is best for you.

Make this experience your own as you move in and out of Universal Heart Meditation, Somatic Listening, and Creative Exploration at your own pace. Be authentic to your own practice and allow your own patterns and methods to emerge. Begin to notice in everyday life how Earth is present with you and how you sense it as an intelligent force that is familiar in it's connection to your mind, body, and soul.

CHAPTER FOUR

Water – Flow with Eternal Freedom

"If we don't have water, we don't have a life or a future."
Máxima Acuña

Imagine the Universe as a never-ending ocean of radiant cosmic space connecting all that is. Our souls swim within this ocean of oneness, this home, as part of the Source of Life. The Source of Life moving through all that is—as the intelligence of Universal Love—pervading our bodies, planet, solar system, galaxy, and continuing throughout the interstellar multiverses.

ONE HEART JUSTICE

Water is a manifestation of this Source—as an element within our bodies, planet, other planets, and space itself. The subatomic particles in planet Earth's water along with the water in our bodies, resonate with the Source of all as a conduit of life and freedom. We can attune to Water through sacred sounds, words, and actions—creating a relationship of mutual honor with Water that brings great joy. Water offers its particular wisdom to those open to becoming Waterkeepers.

True of all elements: Water is a manifestation of love. Water says, *I am in you and I embrace you. I am both visible and invisible. I am flowing, permeable, expansive, and interconnecting.*

Today, as this is written, snow and ice have fallen. I attune with them, feeling them as a conduit of loving change. As weather, Water delivers information from different parts of the Earth. You may ask the Water of your local weather to allow you to integrate the information it brings you and notice what you think and feel in response. Listen, and Water will show you how different parts of the Earth work together to bring vibrancy and balance to the whole planet, through storm systems and earth channels. Attuning with Water as weather, you can send messages of health, vitality, and balance to Water in your physical vicinity to carry through and around the globe. As the natural systems of Water become out of balance due to human disconnection, Water as weather becomes increasingly fierce: in both torrential storms, and lacking, in places where it was once abundant.

Even in past times of greater balance Water was not always gentle. Water can be dangerous, vast, and powerful. It calls for great respect and an acknowledgment of our vulnerability and mortality. Water is not our enemy, nor is it a force to be suppressed, polluted, or underestimated. Water asks to be engaged through our day-to-day life as well as through modern science and technology—with an understanding of its inherent intelligence.

Water consciousness carries the essence of flow throughout the greater system. Bond with Water in your daily life and you will feel it giving back to you through shared intention. Engage Water with the gratitude it deserves as a loving intelligence, and it returns this energy to you, amplifying the field of synergistic consciousness. In this way, Water is a profound teacher and is guiding us toward the fulfillment of our potential to live in sacred union—with our bodies, the Earth, and the Universe.

Imagine a calm pond, still, reflecting the sky's light. Feel the interconnected life buzzing within this pond and hold it in your heart. This is harmony washing through us as elementary particles. Allow the essence of Water to move through your body and let it form a sphere around you. Close your eyes and feel your body come alive with rejuvenation. Engaging in visualization with Water can help us feel revitalized, through our imagination as a healing force. You can also listen to music that carries the emotional tone and message you desire—focus on the sound permeating and vibrating the Water in your body.

Recognizing and nourishing Water as a part of ourselves connects our hearts, minds, and bodies to all the Water in our lives. It allows us to listen beyond the noise of human society to the presence of Water. This listening allows us to better gauge when we are using too much, to wonder where our Water comes from beyond our faucets, and to deeply care about the health of our Water, as we would a member of our family. The pollution of our rivers, lakes, streams, oceans, ponds and aquifers can be reversed when approached with nourishing hearts

ONE HEART JUSTICE

and minds integrating science and technology with a conscious reverence for Water. Many people have and continue to take action in this manner with passion, undaunted by the enormity of the task and undeterred by paradigms and systems of consumption and pollution.

We join the Waterkeepers by focusing on the vision of vital Waters. There are many ways to participate in taking care of Water to reduce toxic run off, pathogens, bacteria, microplastics, lead, and other chemical pollutants. Water emphasizes that connecting with it as a living being—a singular consciousness—is an important practice in order to create change that will last. Water asks us to reconnect our consciousness with the sacred awareness of interbeing and reminds us to value it fully. It is effective to take time to value ourselves, our lives, our connection to the Source of all things and our precious time here on Earth, with Water and other life forms.

Water does not guilt or shame us. As a messenger close to the Source of Life, it guides us through the glint of itself shining in the sun—sending love to humanity. Water says, *I am ready to be honored, so I may fully honor you and all beings.* This reciprocal, sacred relationship is one of love. It is with love we see the most polluted waters and choose to listen to the possibilities of restoration. Guilt and fear will only continue to limit us in our scope of imagined solutions. It is love that opens our beingness to the inclusive sphere of knowledge and wisdom. Allow the sound of Water to come into your open heart and listen with ears that hear deep spirit. What does Water say to *you*?

Awareness perceived as love is the unifying force of focus and empathy. Engaging Water in contemplative and creative practice allows us to give and receive with it. As we integrate this awareness into our daily lives and societies we move toward a shift in global culture. When I engage in this way, I hear Water saying that humans embody unique possibilities to effect change, through the choices of intention and attunement. I see this potential as similar to the infinitely diverse molecular patterns of snowflakes. Each person interconnects fully, in unique expression, enlivening the whole with vitality and nondual awareness, amplifying both individuality and interconnection.

Research on the quantum properties of Water as it responds to sound and electromagnetic vibration, reveals a symmetry of resonance between humanity and the living systems which sustain us. When we see that Water is a living presence, we understand it wants to be engaged intentionally by us. Developing a new approach to Water, we speak with our presence: that Water serves all of life on this planet, not only humans. As a conduit of Universal Love, Water seeks a deeper relationship with humanity. Water offers channels for peace when engaged as a global resource, with the capacity to unify us in developing solutions for sustainable care across all forms of boundaries. Water seeks to teach us how to align societal systems with natural resources and intricate ecological and microbiological structures. As we listen, corporate, political, and economic structures will continue to shift toward true ecological justice. Water has a powerful voice, and the way to hear it is through love—love for all manifestations of Water itself, all people, the whole planet, all beings. Love is a unifying force, the true presence of all things. Love opens the way for Water to come rushing, saying, *there is so much I want to teach you.*

The more one engages with Water from a deep heart and mind connection, the more noticeable Water's sentience becomes, on a visceral level. As I engage in Universal Heart Meditation today, Water is present in my awareness as the

ONE HEART JUSTICE

Ocean. Waves of powerful love wash into me and back, through the planetary spirit and beyond. For each of us, increasing our connection with Water will bring unique insights, experiences, and actions. Engaging in contemplative communion amplifies Water's voice in the realms of humanity. I feel Water guiding this shift in awareness as an invitation to choose expansion of nourishment and respect. Water is both gentle and powerful. It seeks to awaken us to a greater existence, both within and around us. Follow Water's freeing stream with gratitude, reverence, and belief, and allow a journey to unfold. It may take you into deeper love with yourself. Look into the pool of your own eyes in solemn reverence, with Water's song—a song that sings Water alive, making even its invisible presence dance.

Receiving the presence of Water is deeply personal. It moves me to tears. It is coming home to a way of being much of the world has moved away from as we drift in our connection from the natural world. There are many choices available in responding to the call to reconnect with Water in a sacred way. I hear Water encouraging me to enliven this way of being in this moment. Bring this sacred knowing into the heart of your own modern life and see what happens. This is a great experiment—to weave a deep connection with Water into the hustle and bustle of daily life. As I walk around attuning to Water, at once I feel it everywhere, and I become curious about learning more about local Water sources. I feel Water vibrating in all things, in the holy bodies of the people passing by me. I imagine the network of pipes underground and the sources of local Water and feel gratitude for the people caring for Water in my town. I begin to wonder how a spiritual approach to Water can influence current economic and political structures.

As we come together to generate solutions, transforming human systems that denigrate Water and all of Earth's living elements, Water asks us to love one another. Water offers an instructive vision: to weave our ways through the spaces between the boulders of corporations, world leaders, and obstacles in our own minds, to form a force born of passion for Water. Indigenous peoples are leading the way in protecting the elements of Earth, globally. And Water asks all of humanity to feel the absolute necessity of it's presence—vital to our own existence.

Our lives depend on Water, and I hear it saying: *I wish to hear my name on the lips of humanity as often as the utterance of money.* Water shows me that humanity has imagined a global financial system based on misconception. Water seeks to be a lead character in a new mythos, created and enacted by humanity at large. This is more than a paradigm shift of the mind. Water says open your heart, soul, and full body wisdom to the truth of life on this planet and a narrative based on sacred balance will emerge. Water reminds us that the flow of Universal Love is the true economy. The primary elements of life, including Water, support humanity in reweaving the flow of resources, through loving and valuing the source of life itself, and seeing each aspect of life as equally deserving of reverence and developmental nurturance.

Water acknowledges its pervasive pollution by plastics, non-biodegradable chemicals, pathogens, and other forms of human waste. It asks us to connect with its vitality and ability to transform. Water seeks to partner with humanity to generate ways of interacting that nourish its natural state of health so that it can deliver the nurturance it desires to provide. When we prioritize the restoration of our Waters, many hopeful solutions, currently known and ready to emerge, will flourish.

Water reminds us that it is primarily fear, in the forms of greed and selfishness, that are preventing a greater shift in the healing of Water. Water asks us to temper our fear, and our anger, with love for each other, disentangling us from the dominant patterns of power and control.

Water confirms that storms are increasing in intensity and frequency and asks us to understand these are not acts of revenge. Water offers us an opportunity to connect to the landscapes where we live, to set aside more land for Water to find a safe home, and to make channels for Water to circulate with the least amount of damage to humans, other animals, and ecosystems. It is time for us to wake up from avoidance inside our human-made distractions and reconnect with the necessity and power of Water and all of the elements of life.

Water can help us shift from fear to peace when we experience the soothing sound of waves rolling onto shore, as we breathe deeply. We experience our bodies in a state of peace and envision that peace as mist soaking into the whole planet. Water asks us to study the places where it is yet vital and largely unpolluted. Paying close attention to how Water engages with surrounding life in the healthiest ecosystems will provide guidance for how to restore health to Water in the most damaged environments. When in balance, plants, animals, and the land itself shift and adapt to support each other. They are intuitively aware of their interconnections, listening to and caring for one another. As you choose to listen to Water, as a sentient being you will know through the feeling in your heart and the wisdom enlivened in your body the truth being shared. Water speaks to me through guiding images in my mind, words of encouragement, and feelings of love and hope, even in my lowest moments. It gives me courage and reminds me that even the saliva with which I speak is allied with the great power of its life-giving spirit. To actively reconnect with Water as a daily practice, and speak to and for Water, is an honor we can all choose to step into. Water will empower you.

As I tune in with today's rain, forecasted for days, Water draws me up into the clouds and into the broader patterns of weather. Weather around the globe is seeking to maintain homeostasis for the whole. I ask this rainstorm, *what do you need?* Water shows me: too much pavement and continued development with little consideration to Water's best health. What is best for Water is best for all. Commonly, we perceive these rainy days as an inconvenience in places where Water is not scarce. Water asks us to perceive rainfall with gratitude and to increase our awareness of the essential hydrologic cycle of groundwater—evaporation—rainfall. Water reminds us of its sacred union with plants and forests. Cities and towns interspersed with an increase of plants, micro forests, and streams are a path forward. Hydrologists, ecologists, naturalists, and other caretakers of our natural world are aware of these solutions and more.

I ask Water how listening and engaging with it as a singular, sentient being in multiple forms is beneficial for people already devoted to studying and advocating for Water health. Water says many humans honor their connection with Water through passion and service, and asks that they be open to receiving and imparting gratitude and resilience in continuing a sacred partnership. Water tells me again of its deep love for humanity as children who have grown, who have become disconnected from the natural world of which all is made, and who are developing values that call them home to honor Water and all of life.

Water will welcome you home with full embrace and give you gifts of adaptability and transformation as you accept its

ONE HEART JUSTICE

energy into your body in contemplation and celebration. I ask Water to show me how to transform my way of life, what actions to take on a micro and macro level to contribute to its health and wellbeing in my community, country, and the greater globe. Water tells me to start with truly acknowledging it throughout my day—when I bathe, cook, drink; turn off the faucet to conserve, and vote. Water asks us all to hold its sacred spirit in our hearts. Being in spirit connection with Water as we take action for conservation and protection is an important practice.

One morning, when I am struggling with fears about my life, my children, and the state of the world, and question *am I doing enough?* I attune with Water. Water again brings me to look into my own eyes with compassion. I *am* a body of Water being nourished by the great spirit of Water. As I drink my morning coffee and eat oatmeal, I reflect on Water's guidance to be open-hearted and receive love. Water in my coffee, water in my food, water supporting the healing of this cold virus…Water supports my expression of being enough, through receiving and giving love.

Water reminds me not to worry about what is outside of my control but to choose to radiate love throughout all of creation. Water says it is a great vehicle for this meditation, as it pervades every form of life on the planet. Water teaches me not to just radiate outward but to radiate as *part of.* Water gives me an image of its strength, the power of its current, and asks me to allow this strength into my body. I feel renewed hope and believe in promising possibilities. Water is showing me how to harness its strength in reciprocal ways that are life-giving.

Water brings the way we grow food and raise animals for consumption to my awareness. Water acknowledges the industrialization of these processes on a large scale as major sources of pollution in the form of runoff of feces and pesticides. Water says large scale irrigation is wasteful and unnecessary. Water shares that the movement of love and valuing of Water brings awareness to the imbalance in the economic and corporate paradigms that cause agricultural and other forms of Water pollution. As more of humanity shifts to prioritizing care for all aspects of life, these seemingly impenetrable systems will adapt. Water says true leaders in this movement acknowledge Water as a sentient and powerful entity in its own right. Protecting Water, driven only by the motivation of human need, is another form of fear, and the outcome will bring further imbalance. Water brings loving awareness to interconnection and says *let love flow* with the strength of its most powerful rivers. Those who doubt love's power as a catalyst for solutions, who perceive love's path as naive, have not yet experienced its true capacity for transformation and its penetrating intelligence.

Water brings my attention to the animals that depend on its health and abundance for survival, and the fish and other water species that are impacted by life-altering changes to their ecosystems. Water wants us to deeply consider the impact human choices have on all species connected to it. Water illuminates the fact that all creatures, other than humans, instinctively develop biological functions and ways of life that guard against compromising the health of Water. I ask Water: *how have humans lost this connection and prioritization of it?* Water shows me a gradual global disconnect by much of humanity from the importance of the sacred treatment of Water. Water has progressively been perceived as a means to advance human society, with declining connection to it as a vital source of life whose health is absolutely intertwined with that of human development and all other forms of life. The severity of this detachment is causing devastating levels of damage to Water and other foundational resources of creation and makes it impossible for humans to remember their interconnection with Water. Water reminds us it does not seek our pity, our fear, or arrogance; it waits openly to be engaged with love and reverence.

Water points to the daily practice of recognizing it as part of who we are, honoring ourselves and giving thanks to Water, knowing it can feel this. Water asks us to get information about where it resides in the places we live, and what its quality of health is. Water tells us to ask what it needs.

It will answer, showing us with images, body sensations, and a soft voice of words. Each relationship with Water is unique, and Water shares that a diverse ecosystem is healthy. The diversity of the relationships we each have with Water is a necessary part of reconnecting with and restoring Water as an essential component of life. Water teaches me what a reciprocal relationship of love celebrating creation feels like. It shows me the eternal flow of life we have access to beyond all societal limitations. I hear Water splashing with joy and feel called to cultivate the kind of relationships children have with Water as an intelligence to be revered like a trustworthy elder—an elder full of vitality, wisdom, and nourishment with many stories to tell, skills to teach, and cautions to instill.

Water next brings my awareness to glacial melting. I immediately feel grief, and Water says *yes, it is a loss.* Water asks me not to get stuck in my grief and to follow its path as it moves from ice to water and flows in new ways. Water says we must embrace the changing landscape and become stewards of the shift. We will find ways to create healthy, albeit radically different, landscapes as we honor and listen to the elements of the ecosystems we are a part of. Water emphasizes we must be ready to be flexible and reminds us that working for survival has the power to bring humanity together. Look to our young people emerging as leaders to restore ecological balance and see the passion and bravery born of love that moves them.

Water has deep guidance for humans enduring the transformation of grief. Water extends compassion for the physical, emotional, and psychological pain of grief. It lends its spirit to help us feel held during the intense waves of early grief—the kind of loss that feels as if your insides are disintegrating and your heart is broken. Water reminds us to breathe through these waves of grief and to witness them as they begin to ebb. This is how Water helps us know we will survive. We survive, are forever transformed, and even thrive again as we allow grief to ebb and flow like Water. We release control and find we are truly held in Universal Love. Water shares that it takes time to allow the experience of loss to ease in intensity. All the Elements and the Source of Life can support us through grief. Water offers its soft flow to inspire our endurance, just as streams erode rock and create new paths. Grief can be shocking, intense, and flow for lifetimes. Water encourages us to stay in the flow of grief, to stay present to our own and others' grief. Within this experience, we shed tears and find release and nourishment, allowing storms of grief to pass through us, eventually bringing moments of gratitude when the sun breaks through the clouds and we feel hope and love. We find our hearts expanded and our resolve to go on strengthened. Our sense of life beyond the death of our bodies becomes illuminated, just as Water changes form, from solid to gas. Water says: *stand at my ocean and know this is a drop in the field of Universal Love that we rejoin as we transition from body to spirit.*

I ask Water how it can soothe us in grief when it causes so much human grief through flooding, storms, tsunamis, and drownings? Water responds by saying it is open to collaboration for how to be less harmful to human life. It reminds me it has to respond to all of Earth's changes, from earthquakes to conditions related to global warming increasing storm severity. Water would like to become more balanced, in mutual respect with humanity. It guides us to deeply understand: Water is one of the most powerful and foundational aspects of life on Earth. It reminds us to be humble and grateful for our lives and aware of our mortality. Water shares that humanity's defenses against accepting our lack of control over our own mortality prevent us from understanding what is most important to sustain our own lives and other forms of life on Earth. Water says humans must learn to value our own lives, and each other's, equally, as well as thinking and feeling beyond our fear of death. This psychological, emotional, and spiritual balance will open us to acknowledging the need to revere Water and to support those who are creating healthy ecosystems for all— Water systems that protect the health of Water, the lives of humans and other animals, and the fullness of life as a whole on the planet. Water says collaborating with it will be different for each person, but it helps to acknowledge it as a living being in our consciousness and not an object to be manipulated. We underestimate the intelligence of Water when we approach it as an object and minimize the potential of Water to show us best ways to work with it innovatively.

Water has a great deal to tell us about how to create and protect channels for it, over and through Earth, that can be shifted easily to adjust to seasons, guiding Water to the places where it can create the most symbiotic benefits. Water speaks to me about rising temperatures and increased evaporation diminishing great bodies of Water globally, and says we are not utilizing rainwater enough to replenish humanity's Water supplies. Water emphasizes we need to shift our understanding and develop daily practices that include mass collection of rainwater and creating channels that help maintain large bodies of Water. If we engage Water reservoirs and bodies of Water with sensibilities that truly reflect Water's value, we will allocate the resources necessary to protect and restore it. Water brings my awareness to practices such as cloud seeding, which uses technologies to induce rain in certain areas of drought. Water says we are moving in the wrong direction if we are not thinking globally and working across borders to redistribute Water supplies and adjust where and how we love. Practices such as cloud seeding can become divisive between peoples, regions, and countries, perpetuating competition for resources.

Water again brings my attention to how cultivating nonjudgmental, compassionate love for ourselves and extending this lovingkindness to those closest to us, radiating it outward to our neighbors and onward toward all people and all of life, helps us to reconnect our consciousness with the value of life itself. Valuing life, we stand in the presence of love to adjust and create holistic systems that value each aspect of life, equally. Water shows itself as a manifestation of bonding through equity. It shows us how compassion is the true economy and deserves the greatest value—to be our greatest priority. What we value, Water reminds us, flourishes.

Water has more to say about the current of money. The Universe can be conceptualized as being made from the Void, the presence of life becoming aware of itself and expanding through Universal Love. Love alone can create wealth that is shared equally. Love is distributed throughout the Universe connecting all that is. Our experience of Water on Earth points

ONE HEART JUSTICE

to the power of currency: many molecules working together, many hearts and hands working together, guided by individual intelligence and respect for the one and the all. We *are* love, says Water. When we listen, our consciousness of the love we are expands, and the presence of love itself becomes an ocean, expanding to the point of fullness. Water says human evolution is poised to increase our collective consciousness of Universal Love, toward a global shift toward unity. This embodiment and action toward universal interconnection, through the currency of equity, care, and expansion of universal awareness, is part of all that is reaching its fullness.

Water allows us to begin to understand this concept as the circulation of resources, perceived as love, and flowing within humanity and beyond humanity, becoming the Source of Life itself. Life as Cosmos, the physical manifestation of Universal Love, partners with Water in the physical and spiritual realms, reminding us we all deserve to be in the flow of abundance, health, equity of development, and safety. All of life deserves equal resources to support existence and transformation, to thrive in fullness, *as love*, to the fullest extent possible. Water instructs us to believe in love and the universal truths of life to redistribute wealth toward restoration and reconstruction of systems, integrating all we know with true care and space to grow. To generate the equal distribution of true wealth, Water asks each of us to see our own reflection with nonjudgmental eyes, to appreciate who we are and the lives we have lived. Water proclaims that justice is owning our own lives, with deep love and reverence for ourselves as we are and extending that love to all else. Water teaches us to feel into it as an eternally flowing spiritual being to understand how our own souls are part of this never-ending flow of freedom.

This is our primary purpose as humans: to love ourselves, others, and all of life unconditionally. As humans, until we find compassion and empathy for even the worst aspects of ourselves and others, we create many barriers and distractions, keeping us from love. Compassion combined with truth of inquiry creates true solutions. Water says: *live fully, whatever that means to you, and allow your unique intelligence to flow through your heart and permeate your body, soul, and the spirit of all.* This is how we survive, strive, and support one another toward true wealth—where money becomes aligned with the intelligence of Universal Love and is imbued with the true meaning of wealth, which is shared love inside the landscape of life. Water says: *fall into me, to loving life through your breath and presence.*

Water has more to say about justice and demonstrates through its unifying presence on Earth and throughout the Cosmos its equal care for all of life. Water reflects that when we don't fully honor our own and others' true value due to societal pressures, we forget the truth of creation: that we are all reflections of the one Source of life. When we attempt to protect ourselves at the expense of others, we equally harm ourselves. Water says power and control are illusions of safety that harm both those who take them up, and those who are oppressed by them. Water asks us to allow it to wash away bias, prejudice, assumptions, misperceptions, and urges to misuse power whenever we become aware of these experiences within our own consciousness. Water provides support to people suffering due to oppression and injustice, struggling with intergenerational trauma, lack of resources and marginalization. It offers strength in its spiritual form, to endure, to find joy, and to thrive in harsh circumstances by enlivening its presence in our bodies. It shares our reflection as beings of wisdom, beauty, and light; and that however this truth is being obscured is irrelevant to the force of life, the Source of love, and the eternal truth of wholeness.

Water calls us to collective action through continuous transformation and healing of our consciousness, to nourish ourselves and one another as it nourishes us. It understands the embodiment of rage as the torrent of force to push back, to make space, to claim equity. Water supports us in harnessing our rage *at* injustice, individually and collectively, so that we do not take it out on ourselves and others. Water calls us to pay attention to the ways our experiences of injustice intersect and overlap and diminish our mutual ability to thrive. Water radiates the truth that human misuse of power extends beyond our harming of each other and ourselves and is the cause of major devastation to our planet. So many of us are both oppressed and privileged simultaneously, within systems established and maintained through dominance and a misconception of true power. Some of us are marginalized and oppressed to the fullest extent, demonstrating the brutality that emanates from human consciousness that is separated from the truth of interbeing. Water recommends we each find the best path of safety and love possible, with those who care and are willing to dive deeply into personal and communal growth and commitment to ride the waves of life, with Universal Love as our guide.

Water lets us know the flow of life is equal for all humans and all beings, and that in order to shift our societal systems toward equity of resources and thriving development for all humans and all of life we need to experience more compassion for ourselves and others. Compassion and right action cultivate justice. Water is a great teacher of compassion—through visualization or the physical experience of soothing streams, floating, drinking and being nourished by Water. Water expands our sense of interconnectivity through its large bodies and interstellar presence. When we engage contemplatively and physically with Water, it shows us that prioritizing quality of life for all people can create the safety, trust, and healing we seek. Systems that maintain poverty and environmental racism, as well as other injustices, impede quality of life for all. Water shares its intelligence, guides itself to where it is needed most, and humanity can harness this adaptivity as opposed to impeding it. Water says when one part of the system is struggling, that is where the resources should flow. Strength, power, and innovation are present and ready to flourish in full diversity among marginalized peoples and populations. Water asks us to understand that each molecule is essential in its contribution to the function of its wholeness—just as each human being is essential to the diverse tapestry of humanity's entire potential. Water calls us to care for and adapt to one another, while maintaining our own integrity.

When I sit in meditation beside the river today, I hear Water say that drought, increased storm severity, rising acidity, temperatures, and sea levels add tension to our relationship with it and are evidence that much of what has been altered cannot be easily restored. Glaciers melting, evaporating rivers, encroaching flood plains, increasingly polluted water all must be adapted to so that we can prevent ecosystems from further deterioration. Water reminds me there are more than enough resources to support each person, animal, and ecosystem if we shift our priorities toward a global conceptual sensibility that considers all of life. Water shared through true intention of multi-beneficial policies, systems and practices—rather than the current socio-economic, geopolitical power dynamics—establishes trust and eco-political principles based on cooperation as opposed to fear and dominance. Water models disregard for human-created boundaries and weaves its networks around the Earth. Water reminds us it is vast on this planet and is the very reason we know what our "blue planet" looks like from outside our own atmosphere.

Anxiety, stress, judgmentalism, and aggression all provide daily reminders to attune to the flow of life. Water reminds me to align myself with the flow of Universal Love, that is eternally unfolding, each moment. It says it can help us to heal our personal traumas through sound meditation, and by engaging it creatively through all of our senses. Listening to the powerful crash of waves, the steady flow of waterfalls, and the trickle of streams, we can find support. Letting the sounds vibrate through our bodies and go wherever they are needed brings relief, deep relaxation, and letting go. Water understands how to loosen internalized experiences in the form of tension and wash them back into eternal oneness. Listen to recorded Water sounds, sit by a stream, go to the ocean, Water is ready to provide us with healing when we feel as though we can't take any more. This morning, allowing the sound of ocean waves to wash through my body and find the places I am holding onto previous emotional, psychological pain gives me the opportunity to be less activated by situations that send my brain and body into overreaction. Accepting healing from Water opens me further as a conduit of Universal Love.

Through sound, visualization, immersing ourselves in, and drinking clean Water, we are sharing a process of healing with Water. Our physical, emotional, psychological, and spiritual healing, individually and collectively, is an essential part of what will restore Water to full health and vitality. We decrease aggression and violence toward ourselves and others, and space opens for new ways to collaborate. We find strength in peaceful connections and find fulfillment in a sense of wholeness. Water urges us to protect ourselves and each other from the ways it can harm us.

Water wants us to know it is safe to feel love and joy—to know and to celebrate that there is enough of what we each need, and we can continue to be as generous with resources as Water is to us.

I know I have fully connected with Water when I have a sensation of sacred union that moves me to tears, and I receive clarity and nourishment. I hear a unifying tone ringing all of the Waters of Earth and beyond into a state of communion. Water and I invite you to embody the practice of reconnection with Water through the One Heart Justice process.

ONE HEART JUSTICE PROCESS
Universal Heart Meditation

Visit Oneheartjustice.com for guided meditation recording of One Heart Justice process

To begin the Universal Heart Meditation, bring your whole body into awareness and allow whatever needs to dissolve into the void of nothingness to release and fade away. Breathe into this dissolution state and relax into stillness. When you are ready, allow the source of life to emerge through your heart center and breathe deeply into your heart. As you exhale, know that you are in connection with the one source of all creation. Feel your heart spark with the intelligent life force causing it to beat. Allow the spark of life's source to alight in each of your energy centers moving up to your throat center, your third eye center, crown center and up above your head rooting into the source of life. Bring your awareness back down through each energy center and feel the spark of source life energy to blossom in your solar plexus center, your belly center, root center and down into your feet and below you rooting into the source of life. Remember you are created of this one magnificent source, illuminating your heart, all of you, and all the innumerable manifestations of creation on Earth and beyond.

From your radiant heart center, and all of your energy centers you can envision and feel this loving source intelligence radiating out from your body, until you are fully residing in a sphere of unconditional love. Stay here for a moment and soak in love as if you are a plant soaking in light.

As you experience the awareness of your whole body within the sphere of universal love, you can allow this energy to continue to expand in all directions, radiating further and further, as far as your sensory awareness and imagination will expand, until you know that you have expanded fully. Feel the love of the universe coming back toward you, enveloping your expansion in a hug, and know that you are fully interconnected with the web of life. From this place, born of the source of all of creation and connected through the force of love, you can begin to listen, ask for guidance, share and receive information.

Hold the spirit of Water in your heart, your mind, and your body. Be present with whatever arises. As always, if this feels uncomfortable, you may try shifting from fear to curiosity. If you begin to feel overwhelmed in any way, take a break from the practice and engage in self soothing and getting support. When contemplating Water feels right, continue into Somatic Listening.

Somatic Listening

As you move into Somatic Listening and listen with your whole body by being nonjudgmentally aware of body sensations, images, words, cognitive impressions, and emotional tones, imagine these are ideas allowing you to learn with Water. If you lose focus, bring your awareness back to you heart center and smile, feeling the presence of Water in your heart as you breathe and regain focus. Notice what sensations, images, emotions, and words draw your attention most and feel powerful to explore further. Ask Water what messages it has for you to deepen your understanding of how to engage in the flow of eternal freedom. Allow the spirit of Water to illuminate your crown energy center or any other energy center that feels right. As you hone in on impressions to transition into creative exploration with, take a moment to make notes or draw in your journal, or amplify body sensation into movement, or sound. Use whatever ways seem most effective to bring expression and understanding to your Somatic Experience with Water that is the right way for you today.

Creative Exploration

As you move into the third aspect of the creative contemplation process, Creative Exploration, know that you can return to the Universal Heart Meditation and Somatic Listening at any time, and then back into Creative Exploration.

Your expressive arts practice can be in any artistic medium. You may choose to take your sensory experience into movement, visual arts, sound, or music. You can also focus on a problem you are solving, a current project, a relationship you are in process with and ask Water to support you with new approaches and ideas. The wisdom you gain in contemplation with Water is yours to create with in whatever way that is best for you.

Make this experience your own as you move in and out of Universal Heart Meditation, Somatic Listening, and Creative Exploration at your own pace. Be authentic to your own practice and allow your own patterns and methods to emerge. Begin to notice in everyday life how the Water is present and how you can sense it as an intelligent force that is familiar in it's connection to your mind, body, and soul.

CHAPTER FIVE

Air – Share Equity of Space

""In out, Deep slow, Calm ease, Smile release, Present moment, wonderful moment."

- Thich Nhat Hanh

Air, full of oxygen, formed from the ocean, entering us, just as we emerge from warm water to take our first breaths. I imagine the complexity of invisible gasses surrounding Earth, relish a deep breath, and feel woven into the fabric of existence.

We often move about in Air without a second thought, until it wakes us up to it's presence as a light breeze or chilly

ONE HEART JUSTICE

wind. Air calls us to acknowledge its invisible necessity to us, as breathing creatures.

I listen to Air, honor it, appreciate its life-giving support. Being with Air turns my head to the sky and opens my heart to possibility. I am grateful for its life-sustaining presence at different altitudes, allowing myriads of forms to exist and move about. Geese fly overhead; I consider their ancient nature, how in this moment they point toward protection for all creatures.

Considering Air as a universal being expands my imagination beyond Earth's atmosphere into the vacuum of outer space, where Air becomes space itself.

In meditation I feel into the universal expanse, the innumerable galaxies, the possibility of life on other planets. I feel my consciousness expand, deepen, evolve in understanding that humans have the opportunity to behold the space of the entire Universe in sacred reverence. Our ability to perceive life with wonder and awe is a catalyst for bringing greater health to our present time. Holding the intention of unity on our planet can allow us to move through space connecting with people working toward vibrant connection. Increased experience of the sacred nature of space itself, propels us from a dying planet for our species to a thriving planet ready to engage in new dimensions of understanding.

This morning I do the Universal Heart meditation, and I feel the eternal presence enlivening my heart and radiating throughout my body, the planet, and into the expanse. Presence with my breath puts me in contact with the intelligent force of life. It reminds me of a theory in physics…about dark matter being *information* that has mass. I wonder about intelligence and information and how to harness the force of life for the good of all, within my own being.

Air shows me its embrace—it surrounds me and permeates me, as well as soil, water, and other creatures. Air offers me an opportunity to attune to the eternal embrace—the one in which the physical transforms through death, yet the information, the soul we are, merges with spirit and continues. Air's message to me today is to focus on the impact we have on each other and the world around us. We all breathe the same Air. Compassion, forgiveness, listening, laughing, understanding are as vital as oxygen to humanity. Through these capacities, we can shift the effects of a global virus, just as we shift the damaging impact we have on each other and the planet—one breath at a time.

Imagining the current quality of Air around the globe, I think about pollutants and the thinning of the ozone. I feel thankful for the protection Air as atmosphere gives us from the sun's radiation and that it has maintained a balance of gasses for so many forms of life to evolve. I feel Air ready to release excess carbon through methods of absorption, utilizing other elements to regain balance and continue in the homeostasis that has been developed through symbiotic relationships. I feel it working in conjunction with soil, trees, plants, and water, calling me to value, contemplate, and understand its interconnectivity more deeply. I ask Air: how can its interconnectivity lead to its healing? Air brings my attention to forest preservation and planting, to techniques in which the soil absorbs excess carbon. I think about factories, farming, fossil fuel industries waking up to the intrinsic benefits of shifting concepts and practices. Feeling the wisdom of Air present within and around me gives me hope that radical shifts can occur within the hearts and minds of people in positions of power and coming generations, to broaden our understanding of how food, transportation, and power will embrace true change, and of how we will find empowerment through transformation.

Air's interconnectivity with every aspect of life demonstrates the necessity of mutual nourishment. It reminds me that we are learning as humans to be less brutal and becoming more nourishing to ourselves and others. As we grow stronger in our ability to love ourselves and others unconditionally, we share sacred respect with all of life; engaging in mutual benefit. Contemplating Air—the balance of oxygen, carbon dioxide, nitrogen, and the other gasses it holds—brings me to focus on how important collaboration is to finding what works for a thriving whole. Restoring the health of Air as we know it requires working together; bridging barriers of fear and denial.

I ask Air to teach me about trust, and it shows me how I rely on Air without thinking. It is always there for me, as I live in a primarily unpolluted region. I trust it will continue to sustain me. Yet I have taken it for granted, grown apart from the reality of its essential nature. I realize that a foundational aspect of trust is value. As I remember to value the very Air I breathe, I easily understand how it important it is for us to develop our ability to value ourselves and each other and all aspects of creation with equal measure.

Being with Air calls me to think in deep time. To understand that even if humanity is not able to recalibrate the environment for our own wellbeing, many life forms will live on, as will Earth itself, for billions of years, continuing to move through phases of vast extinction and evolution. Perhaps what lies ahead are lineages of species we can hardly imagine. Could the dinosaurs imagine humans? To broaden my awareness of Air…to a time before it could support human life, and possibly to a time when it can no longer…expands my consciousness through time and space. Positioning myself in this way, I am filled with hope and curiosity about what is to be done on the personal level to support Air. I wonder how to reconcile feeling overwhelmed by enormous global industrial systems, my personal limitations, and the damage that feels irrevocable.

I admit, as I sit with Air in dialogue, that I feel powerless and culpable, having grown up in an age where I at once feel such deep connection with the natural world around me, including fellow humans, yet I am part of the many systems that have in my lifetime denigrated the entire planet and maintained the status quo. Systems of economic priority, dehumanization, industrial greed and ecological degradation have harmed many forms of life, including members of my human family, in my neighborhood and across the globe.

I feel grateful for leaders in human rights, ecological protection and restoration, those who work to shift agricultural and industrial practices; I value their contributions and guidance in how to move forward. Yet in my heart and soul it does not feel like I can do enough; like so many others, I am unsure about what contributions on a personal level make a lasting difference. So I turn to asking Air itself, and again Air brings me to my breath…my nose and the miracle of smell, the filling of my lungs and exchange of oxygen and carbon dioxide.

Air guides me to feel it as a form of love: to feel sustained, breath by breath; filled with life. Air illuminates the interwoven dimensions, culminating in life—in *my* life. As I breathe deeply, I acknowledge my grief and guilt. I am reminded that Air is not calling me to go to war, to fight my neighbor, to criticize myself. It beckons me to understand: the true power at the root of fear and rage, seeking change, justice, protection, and healing, is love. While demonstrations of love may

ONE HEART JUSTICE

be fierce—transforming consciousness and actions to harness courage, to move toward rebalance of equity for all of life—we must stay attuned to the center, the core, the unified field of love found in the life-giving quality of Air.

Considering the guidance I am receiving when contemplating Plant, I think about my relationship and response to conflict. Recently I have been noticing my sensitivity to what feels harsh and escalating. I'm taking accountability for the pattern of my past interpersonal trauma being activated—my tendency to overreact when I feel people are escalating a situation. In the meditative state with Air, I feel the tension between the temporal and the eternal. The tension feels for a moment like the point of high conflict, the perception in which there are only opposing forces, a right side and a wrong side. Air teaches me to step down internally, to feel space within and around me. Within this space, I find a full, 360 degrees; I can pivot, I can shift from fear and anger to curiosity. I begin to practice feeling the physical, psychological, emotional space within and without. I consider the notion of each person taking up space. Air does not discriminate. We are all equal within the field of Air.

I consider the acts of giving and receiving and imagine all of the movement on the planet—of the planet, the solar system, the galaxy, and beyond—as one being, held together by the space of Air. From this perspective, Air becomes the venue for our individual communication, perception, movement, and expression, as one being within the larger whole. Air asks each of us what we want to express within this universal expanse. From this place, we each inhabit a most unique expression, filled with possibility and choice, just as we are, the tiniest specs of life, from the edges of the universe, looking back on ourselves.

127

We live but a blink, so why not move toward opening our hearts in authenticity to claim our fullness? Taking deep breaths, stretching, visualizing the Air within the body making space for nourishment now, to pass on to those who come after. In a meditative state with Air my body begins to feel more translucent. I feel the Air within and without. I am held up by Air at this moment, I am disappearing into Air. It is this oneness state that fills me with deep love that I know collectively can change our world.

Today, there is a mist in the Air. The combination of water molecules and Air is one of the many combinations of elements that brings variety to both the external and internal worlds. My field of vision shifts to closer range, turning me inward to notice my inner landscape. This is the magic of the mist—as a transition between spaces....

Air shows me its presence in my body, as oxygen bringing nourishment to all of my organs, feeding me at the subatomic level. I am amazed, imagining all of the tiny vessels supporting the orchestration of carrying oxygen throughout my body and moving carbon dioxide out. I wonder about the first Air-breathing creatures. What called a tiny millipede out of the water to land, almost 500 million years ago? I think of the elegant complexity of my body and attempt to feel into the millions of years, from the first Air-breather to now. It makes me curious about what mechanisms within human understanding could allow us to continue polluting Air? Air brings my awareness to narratives of modern society. Our human tendency to weave stories about what is important, carrying us far from the essential truths of our existence. Air reminds me of its giving nature, its presence here for all, in contrast to certain human cultures that have developed from the concepts of power

ONE HEART JUSTICE

through dominance. I understand how this false perception of power has led to the rapid demise of nature, in only several hundred years. Air calls us to ground ourselves in the truth of nature, and in humanity's true purpose: as stewards of our planet and not destroyers.

This morning as I meditate with Air, I am having difficulty concentrating. In my frustration, I ask Air, *what do you want us to know?* I hear Air reply: it is a vehicle for peace. I ask Air what this means...I have images in my head of the strong winds from the winter storm that downed trees and knocked out power for family and friends just a few days ago. My mind is brought to the globe in its entirety and the Air patterns conducted by hot and cold temperatures. I picture the arcs and spirals Air is orchestrated into. I realize that I think of peace as stillness. Air broadens my understanding of peace as acceptance of how the force of life moves. To be alive, there is always movement and change, as in wind. At times the force of life feels as destructive and chaotic as a hurricane. Wind reminds me of something I learned from past teachers about the eye of the hurricane: honoring the process of allowing fear, anger, and grief to bring us back to grounded presence and deep connection. The deadly gust becomes a soft breeze. I let go of wrestling my own trauma, my need to be right, my drive for control. As much as I resist the truth, I am often brought back to my breath to help me transform my own rage and anger, and my body, my presence, once again feels like an instrument of peace and healing. I am stronger for this process; the one in which I am desperate, at my limit, and find my center of calm again. Air asks us not to give up on ourselves and our struggles and not to give up on Air as an ally.

Air does not discriminate. Air allows all forms of life, for each individual human, to be present in wholeness. Air brings my awareness to the damage that arises from inequality in our current societies, among people, globally. Air shows me how trauma and violence emerge from oppressive systems. Disease increases in systems out of balance between people and the rest of nature. Air says it is free for all creatures, just as resources of food, shelter, medicine, education, and opportunities to share and be compensated for one's gifts need to be free and equally accessible for all people. Air highlights humanity's current focus on developing technologies to shift global warming. Air calls us to also invest in the practice of cultivating the human heart—our capacity for empathy, compassion, and forgiveness.

Air creates the milieu for listening: to listen to one another and allow space for all perspectives; to establish trust that we can work together, with mutual respect, toward each other's flourishing. It is when this trust is violated and the peace-seekers are put on the defensive to protect themselves that cycles of degradation continue. As humanity continues to value conflict, to fight with one another, systems of destruction rage on. I tell Air I feel deflated by this cycle, and about how tenuous peace and seeking equality can be. Air reminds me of the choice each creature has: to listen to themselves and others, to respect each other's needs, and to build connection as opposed to division. Air inspires me to feel empowered by this choice, to understand: it is as powerful as the Air we breathe.

Air is broad and complex, a great messenger for new ideas and expansive listening. Air allows vibrations to find connection so that life can be felt and heard. Meditating with Air, I think about sound on Earth, before it was inhabited by hearing creatures. I wonder about the evolution of hearing and speaking. In the beginning, there were only the sounds of the elements, earthquakes, volcanic eruptions, rain, waves. Over billions of years, many species have come and gone, making their unique reverberations through Air. Eventually, humans developed language, perhaps listening to birdsong. Thousands of languages and so many forms of music arose. I wonder what effect there is on our expression through sound when we are cognizant of Air as co-creator. I practice listening with gratitude for Air, as my guide. Experiencing space and sound in this way heightens my awareness of animate and inanimate aspects of my environment and renews my appreciation for the contribution of all things to the soundscape.

I am excited by opportunity and experimentation with sound. I think of my sensitivity to emotional tone and voice as a therapist, often attuning in support with others, through dialogue. I am drawn to practices of chanting and music developed to attune us to universal truths such as creation itself and interweaving us with nature: the power of the drum to enliven and ground us; the native flute's ability to make me feel surrounded by forest; the power of bird calls in late February to immerse me in the feeling of Spring approaching. I consider the auditory range of the typical human ear and the evolutionary audiological theory that we evolved to hear a higher pitch, specifically to hear birds' songs as indicators of safe and thriving environments.

Air allows us to resonate with other aspects of life. A hawk circles overhead, and for a moment I feel we are connected through inner knowing, feeling each other from afar. I consider cultures who have used these moments of resonance in naming the world around them. Intimacy and honor affect the development of language, and reverence is passed on through words. I imagine Air listening to all the languages that have come and gone within humanity and recognizing what it has to teach us. From this perspective, Air emphasizes the power of the spoken word: the opportunity of choice in how we approach each other, how we touch one another with language.

    Air is at once an element that allows us to exist, to hear, to make sound, as well as it is a begetter of storms—the kind we know now, and those yet more fierce, on the horizon of global warming. Our relationship with Air, the words we speak, affect evolution. When we honor Air, exchanges occur to transform our understanding. It is this call and response with nature, this resonance, that is lost when we get drawn into cycles of consumption. There is a way forward in which nature, loving practices, technology, and modern human culture can move forward into balance and innovation that feel appealing and move all of life into a thriving position. I can see us making that music, dancing to it, and making the modern myth of Air compelling enough to save the planet.

    The intricate design of the ear is scrumptious—its pressure balance, crystal formations, and curvature acoustics. Vibrations moving through Air resound off its tiny, inner drum. The ear, a child of Air, developed through the act of listening. Shifting focus from the other sounds in my environment, I listen to Air. I hear the silence of possibility. What sounds, music, and language emerge from the grateful ear, hearing the source of life as Air? What are the movements of the mouth and tongue, speaking with awareness into the living presence of Air, expanding as far as space exists? I say, *I love you*, to myself, to Air, and feel a release through tears. This simple, vulnerable act reverberates through my whole self. Said to Air, this expression of love ripples throughout the pond of existence, opening space for giving and receiving. I wonder how the state of love has contributed to human evolution. Among narratives of competition and oppression, surely love, compassion, empathy, and sharing

ONE HEART JUSTICE

have shown us the way forward. I return to love for myself, for Air, for all that it allows.

Air shows me bodies moving, inspired by space—elevated heart rates, increased oxygen invigorating our minds and bodies. The right to exist and truth of equality that each person embodies is clear. Air reminds us that as representatives of love from the source of life, we must stand strong through storms of oppression, misinformation, manipulation, and continued injustice. Air says just as the force of love created the mutual interconnection that birthed human beings, we must stay rooted in love to work together toward equity, justice, and respect for ourselves, each other, and all of life. I ask Air: how can we know this more viscerally when feeling rage, hopelessness; burnt out by backlash to progress and continued tragedy? Air reminds me of the danger in seeking equity: not to take on oppressive misunderstandings of victory. We become what we fight. Air recommends choosing to *be* justice, *be* respect, *be* the eternal loving power that withstands all manipulation of its purity. Air says: attune to this purity within and resounding through all of life, embrace and be embraced by the presence of Air that makes you, made your ancestors, makes your children. Bring your awareness back to your breath and temper radical change within acceptance, knowing that all you seek, you are. Stay in this place until the ideas, the plan, the art, the expression that is yours to give, comes forth.

Today I am thinking about the nature of symmetry, and how Air might apply to a pattern I notice with regard to expanding consciousness. When I experience a peak moment, embodying the grand expanse of unconditional love and unity, I soon have an experience bringing me into hopelessness, despair, or deep anger at myself. I ask Air about symmetrical and asymmetrical patterns in nature, in Air itself, and how they might relate to the evolution of human consciousness. As I ask, a soaring bird of prey flies overhead, and its shadow moves across the ground nearby, causing me to recognize that existing in physical form we are enlivened by the sun, as love, which also casts shadows of love's opposites. To know love, we must also understand hate. We learn from opposites: to be touched by despair, is to find redemption and hope. Air's composition on Earth of primarily oxygen and carbon dioxide are symmetrical on the molecular level. This combination of gasses and our lungs' capacity to exchange them to keep our bodies nourished and alive is miraculous, yet Air also contains aerosols that can cause us harm. Air nourishes us, but can also harm us, just as we can practice unconditional love, yet can deeply hurt or kill one another. I remember that the universe expresses mathematical elegance as well as paradox. One theory about the creation of the Cosmos and the Big Bang, involves asymmetry. If physical creation of the Cosmos had been symmetrical, equal parts of matter and antimatter would have cancelled each other out. The extra particle of matter versus antimatter, in asymmetry, cracked open the door to existence. The extra particle of matter, leading to the physical world as we know it, can be conceptualized as a moment of choice. Each of us has the choice to find the source of love, even in its very opposite.

Feeling into Air brings me in touch with acceptance, a broadening of presence that embraces paradox. This broad presence holds all aspects as true: our capacity to be both kind and hurtful beings. To discover love in our most flawed tendencies and in the natural world's most brutal forces, is to cycle into the awareness of oneness where transmutation occurs.

ONE HEART JUSTICE

If we imagine pollution of Air as the culmination of actions caused by seeming opposites of loving forces such as greed, carelessness, and denial, the flawed aspects of human tendencies and systems leading to Air pollution can be seen as the physical expression of our own misguided patterns. When we perceive overconsumption, elitism, and ignorance as causal to the aerosols damaging our ability to engage in our fundamental right to breathe freely, solutions may emerge at the center of our individual day-to-day functioning. Connecting to Air with unconditional love, I am reminded to slow down, show kindness, and steady my breathing.

Nourishing ourselves allows us a sense of peace and freedom. This peace we share with each other allows us to let go of that which is not our true nature. Engaging in practices to soothe our own emotional pain and let go of harmful beliefs, to sense our wholeness physically, emotionally, intellectually, and spiritually, we, in a sense, depollute our own consciousness.

Air as the presence of space reflects our true nature, integrating the internal and external, the singular and multidimensional. Air provides us the opportunity through the breath to become instruments of peace and reminds us that peaceful and open minds create restorative solutions and communicate diplomatically to support integrative change. When we do not take responsibility to transform our own angry, spiteful, resentful, dismissive, and disrespectful thoughts and feelings toward people and practices, continuing to cause pollution, we only contribute to the human processes driving the entrenchment of irresponsible, blameful, and shortsighted measures.

Air calls us to find peace, not to fight. To forgive, not to blame. To use the gifts of conscious breathing to embody the intelligence of the source of all things, interconnected as that one source. Air says: I am available, I am yours, I am a messenger of the source of life, showing you the way toward balance and innovation. Contemplating Air provides us with an experience of sacred space in which we can hold one another accountable without participating in dehumanizing those we disagree with.

Today as I contemplate with Air, I feel dense and worn out by all of the different roles I embody in my life and weighed down by the suffering around the globe. I feel enraged and deeply saddened by another war beginning and all of the traumatic loss that could have been avoided. I complete the Universal Heart meditation and feel Air showing me space within my body. It is as if I am being rejuvenated by the space of possibility I hold within. Air shows me how to create space within and around myself so that I can hold a consciousness and energetic presence of peace, hope, love, and possibility.

I have been frustrated by how easily I am affected by challenging situations and emotions in my personal life and the greater world. Air provides me with reassurance that it is helpful to feel emotion, to feel empathy, and to be fully human, engaging in current life. Air also shows me that it provides room for transmutation of despair, anger, guilt, confusion, and other difficult experiences. I feel held up by the support and power of Air for a moment and then deflate with doubt. My doubt is grief for the pain of others, my limitations, and my fear that this practice and the perspective I am cultivating is unrealistic and there will continue to be war and devastation until we humans are gone. Air reminds me: as a manifestation of the source of life, it brings the everyday experience of the eternal into our lives. Eternal love, provided through the space of Air in my body, around me, and encompassing our planet, provides the alchemy to transform pain, doubt, and fatigue into truth of the resilient living spirit that can never be destroyed. Air is the space within Cosmos, the venue for our hearts and minds to create change, returning us to the origin of the source of life, wholeness, and peaceful cohesion. When we visualize the broader space, the wound is buoyed, and we will not get as mired down. The healthy thriving parts are activated and gather round to process the pain.

Air reminds me of its many dynamics when conceptualized as open space, components we breathe, wind, and as outer space, reaching further than we can imagine. Air is filled with the concepts of physics: the curvature of spacetime, gravity, temperature, Air flow and weather patterns. Air encourages me to see the spaces within the human body as milieus for similar processes. Just as many of the components of Air are invisible to the human eye, so are the functions within the body, including emotional experiences, the soul, and consciousness. Air calls me to consider the complexity of its activity on our planet and beyond, and to liken it to the intricacy of our individual functioning. The message from Air is to focus on integration, and to visualize and embody ordered harmony.

It is helpful to study parts of the whole and to deeply understand details, over long periods of time. Toward increasing global harmony, Air points to engaging in practices that help us attune with ourselves physically, emotionally, and soulfully. My mind is drawn to Chinese medicine and the Indian practice of Ayurveda as ancient healing systems founded on observations and experiences of the natural world and harmonizing the body holistically. Air invites us to start with the microcosm each of us are and to bring our awareness to our whole selves. To notice, allow, and feel gratitude for the billions of processes orchestrating miraculously, while letting go of energy, tension, emotions, and thoughts that are ready to be released. We breathe in vital, fresh, life force and soak it in throughout our bodies, locating what feels to be the soul. *What does it look like, feel like within you? Feel your soul, ask it what it needs.* My soul and life source energy feel to be the primary energies animating my body. I feel these energies expanding throughout my internal physical, emotional, and psychological experiences and moving out of my body, uniting with universal spirit. Air calls me and asks me to encourage us all to believe in the soul as a living embodiment of eternal intelligence, carrying us from lifetime to lifetime.

The presence of the soul soothes the paradox of our individual consciousness being simultaneously one with the spirit that is present in all things. Air teaches me: allowing our souls to expand in expression causes us to grow into our human potential. We become more attuned to universal spirit and able to integrate our individuality, with the ability to co-create complex, healthy systems. Fully embodying our souls, we can find our best expression interacting with other people and become better caretakers for our planet.

Air is a thriving entity, stretching throughout the time and space of the physical universe. It is a manifestation of the source and spirit of life, just as each of us are. To contemplate Air in its fully integrative complexity and connect our own souls with the soul of Air, we become one with space universal. Within this space is the eternal presence of life; our souls create love, the interconnective force allowing us to share nourishing wisdom and become more than our individuality. Wisdom is the information, intention, and action closely aligned with the eternal, life-giving source. This direct soul connection with

Air and all essential aspects of life gives us the information and power to heal ourselves and to heal Air, moving back into mutual balance.

In a state of contemplative, embodied connection, I ask Air: how do we heal you? Air and I envision nourishing energy, originating from the source of life, permeating all space, and transmuting that which is harmful and polluting. This energetic shift in conscious orientation can be taken into action through the presence of nourishment. Nourish the soul; create a nourishing environment. Find opportunities to explore what this means in daily life, in relationships, in choices, each moment. Nourishment creates hope, and hope creates change. Air says living from the deep, timeless energy of your soul allows you to provide grounded, focused strength toward valuing clean Air to breathe and to have clarity about what actions are yours to take in the protection and restoration of Air.

Sitting outside under a blue sky in contemplation with Air today my heart and mind are brought to freedom. Air has much to share about the concept and practice of freedom. It brings my attention to its quality of open neutrality. Within its spaciousness I feel the absence of cultural norms and societal pressures. Air does not encourage anarchy, but the recognition that contemporary human perceptions and practices are permeable. Air provides the blank canvas for humanity to transform current modes of thinking, antithetical to the fundamental principle of Air as an equally enlivening force for all humans. Air wants us to embrace freedom for all and a deepening of principles, aligning with the power of nature to provide and not to discriminate among humans. Air is providing connection on the soul/spirit plane to collaborate toward the dissolution of discrimination, fear-based power, and polluting biases. Air says there is room for all human variations. Air is a great messenger of freedom, because it allows us to become; it does not confine us, but creates environments in which to thrive. Air urges us to deeply value our personal freedom, our unique expression, our soulful stance and engagement with who we are, who we were, and who we will be. Air reminds us that individual freedom enlivens the greater good, as each part of the whole is valued, respected, and important to the functioning of the whole. Air reminds us it is part of a dynamic, multifaceted, complex system, representing what is possible for human systems—if we increase attunement, broadly and cohesively, with the elements.

Freedom is an orientation, embodiment, and expression that we can each choose, despite constricting forces. Air demonstrates adaptive evolution within the power of limits and reinforces finding creative solutions. The breadth of Air inspires us to amplify our personal freedom to love, be loved, and exist in fullness. Air invites us to use the open sky of our imaginations to visualize and believe that freedom for all of humanity and all of life is available through systems, including evolved democracy. Through contemplation of the power and potential of Air we can illuminate the shortcomings and barriers within our current societies. Air urges us to stand present in the storms of today, while breathing grounded life into the possibilities of tomorrow.

Over the ocean, on the ferry, between ribbons of land, a tiny white moth flutters about me in gusts of wind; I am amazed by the tiny wonders of life. Wind batters my ears. It is hurricane season. The great messenger of global currents brings news of fierce storms, set to increase due to global warming. I ask Air the best way for humanity to adapt to the increase in severity of storms, tornados, damage to homes, loss of power, loss of lives, occurring and on the horizon. Air says: prepare by

ONE HEART JUSTICE

helping one another. Continue to build towns and cities using engineering to withstand storms, including underground protection. Air says to start with the most vulnerable of people and environments with the least protection and resources, because the deeper solution to global warming is to generate compassion, trust, care, and innovation across all socially manifested divides. Air shares that for those who are willing and able to connect with it as a sacred entity of life, there awaits connection to ideas in answer to seemingly unsolvable situations.

Air reminds me that our current situation is not a crisis of technology but a crisis of consciousness: A separation of our own understanding of ourselves as animals on a planet created from the source of life through billions of years of evolution, in essential connection to the immense diversity of living. Air offers a way to cultivate the consciousness necessary to move beyond the limiting constructs that maintain the status quo of our current awareness. This consciousness has been relegated by patriarchal, colonial powers to the fringes of modern-day cultures through domination and genocide over thousands of years. To globally shift direction away from continuing to damage ourselves and the planet, we have the choice to reengage with the awareness of interdependent consciousness and integrate it back into our collective evolution.

Air as a universal entity models interdependent consciousness cultivated through oneing meditation and creative, heart-based action. Air calls us to connect these states of being through contemplative moments with our modern-day information, technologies, and egalitarian sensibilities. It is an experience of wholeness we seek in the deeper realms of our human psyche. Air reminds us that experience is available here and now, for all of us, and connecting with Air as a fundamental integrative force of space and integrated elemental environment is a dynamically expansive and cohesive, non-dual, unifying experience. As many cultures over the ages have understood, nature is indeed aware, alive, and ready to collaborate with humanity, if we are willing to coevolve with coherence and courage, engaging with the unifying guide of heart-based wisdom. Air provides the expanse for choice, and the process, experience and outcome of shifting our consciousness is held within the grace of our individual unfolding lives.

Air reminds us we are each whole and beautiful beings who matter, and our lives and choices are enough. We can choose to amplify this understanding and offer this awareness to others through increased love.

ONE HEART JUSTICE PROCESS
Universal Heart Meditation

Visit Oneheartjustice.com for guided meditation recording of One Heart Justice process

To begin the Universal Heart Meditation, bring your whole body into awareness and allow whatever needs to dissolve into the void of nothingness to release and fade away. Breathe into this dissolution state and relax into stillness. When you are ready, allow the source of life to emerge through your heart center and breathe deeply into your heart. As you exhale, know that you are in connection with the one source of all creation. Feel your heart spark with the intelligent life force causing it to beat. Allow the spark of life's source to alight in each of your energy centers moving up to your throat center, your third eye center, crown center and up above your head rooting into the source of life. Bring your awareness back down through each energy center and feel the spark of source life energy to blossom in your solar plexus center, your belly center, root center and down into your feet and below rooting into the source of life. Remember you are created of this one magnificent source, illuminating your heart, all of you, and all the innumerable manifestations of creation on Earth and beyond.

From your radiant heart center, and all of your energy centers you can envision and feel this loving source intelligence radiating out from your body, until you are fully residing in a sphere of unconditional love. Stay here for a moment and soak in love as if you are a plant soaking in light.

As you experience the awareness of your whole body within the sphere of universal love, you can allow this energy to continue to expand in all directions, radiating further and further, as far as your sensory awareness and imagination will expand, until you know that you have expanded fully. Feel the love of the universe coming back toward you, enveloping your expansion in a hug, and know that you are fully interconnected with the web of life. From this place, born of the source of all of creation and connected through the force of love, you can begin to listen, ask for guidance, share and receive information.

Hold the spirit of Air in your heart, your mind, and your body. Be present with whatever arises. As always, if this feels uncomfortable, you may try shifting from fear to curiosity. If you begin to feel overwhelmed in any way, take a break from the practice and engage in self soothing and getting support. When contemplating Air feels right, continue into Somatic Listening.

Somatic Listening

As you move into Somatic Listening and listen with your whole body by being nonjudgmentally aware of body sensations, images, words, cognitive impressions, and emotional tones, imagine these are ideas allowing you to learn with Air. If you lose focus, bring your awareness back to you heart center and smile, feeling the presence of Air in your heart as you breathe and regain focus. Notice what sensations, images, emotions, and words draw your attention most and feel powerful to explore further. Ask Air what messages it has for you to deepen your understanding of engaging equity of space. Allow the spirit of Air to illuminate your throat energy center or any other energy center that feels right. As you hone in on impressions to transition into creative exploration with, take a moment to make notes or draw in your journal, or amplify body sensation into movement, or sound. Use whatever ways seem most effective to bring expression and understanding to your Somatic Experience with Air that is the right way for you today.

Creative Exploration

As you move into the third aspect of the creative contemplation process, Creative Exploration, know that you can return to the Universal Heart Meditation and Somatic Listening at any time, and then back into Creative Exploration.

Your expressive arts practice can be in any artistic medium. You may choose to take your sensory experience into movement, visual arts, sound, or music. You can also focus on a problem you are solving, a current project, a relationship you are in process with and ask Air to support you with new approaches and ideas. The wisdom you gain in contemplation with Air is yours to create with in whatever way that is best for you.

Make this experience your own as you move in and out of Universal Heart Meditation, Somatic Listening, and Creative Exploration at your own pace. Be authentic to your own practice and allow your own patterns and methods to emerge. Begin to notice in every day life how Air is present and how you can sense it as an intelligent force that is familiar in it's connection to your mind, body, and soul.

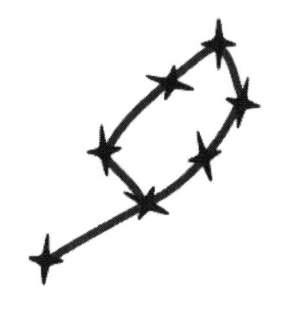

CHAPTER SIX

Plant: Nourish One Another

"In some Native languages the term for plants translates to, 'those who take care of us.'"

- Robin Wall Kimmerer

Earth, water, and sun come together to celebrate the complex beauty of growth through Plants. From the first green cell to the ancient bristlecone pine, Plants have proliferated for millions of years and have much to teach us about coevolution. A confluence of evolutionary events caused a bacterial cell to swallow a cyanobacterial cell, creating photosynthesis; establishing the origin of the first plant: green algae.

ONE HEART JUSTICE

As a spiritual entity in this practice, Plant includes multiple forms of cellular life such as fungi and bacteria, and has much hope humanity will further utilize their multitude of benefits to restore health to the planet while simultaneously cultivating oneness consciousness. As we go forward in this chapter, I will refer to "Plant" as a singular entity, and to "Plants" as the expanded form of that same entity, for they present themselves in just that way: both as a oneness and as a multiplicity.

Plant teaches us how to communicate through mutual support and to create healing ecosystems. They point to the vascular systems of plants and humans as physical replications of universal interconnection. Plant asks us to imagine how the trillions of cells in our bodies interact and to revel in the miraculous nature of our physical form. We are physical, intelligent, and soulful creatures—so are Plants, and all of life. Plant reminds us we experience creative limitations sensorially, and it is wise to broaden our range of perception through contemplation of interbeing and consider the many ways Plants communicate.

Plants hear, see, communicate, and remember through very different biophysiological structures and systems than humans. "Plant" as a Universal Spirit, culminates from individual plants dispersed intergalactically—intelligent beings, eager to continue working with humans to further elucidate how they persevere, proliferate, and drive evolution through the flow of Universal Love. Plant reminds us they have stayed rooted in their evolutionary consciousness to Source energy. They are nature, as are humans, yet human evolution includes a sizable divergence from awareness of universal interbeing. Plants listen, grow, adapt, and change through electromagnetic pulses; fully one with space as an ocean of mostly unidentified particles and forces.

Plant lets us know it is okay that humanity at large has moved away from awareness of our true nature. Plant says, "I am here with you; we are evolving together as creative partners," and reassures us that our individual choices and interbeing consciousness matters. Plant suggests that we allow our bodies and souls to melt into an experience of the void to remind ourselves of the impulse to exist and the natural force of growth. The void can be thought of as nothingness, emptiness, stillness, or neutral space where nothing "exists." Plant teaches us about this fertile space for human renewal that can be explored through somatic contemplation. Plant encourages us to meditate with the void in preparation for working with it on a spiritual level, because it is fertile ground for transformation and Plant can be a model for growth toward interdependent nourishment.

Relaxing into nothingness, Plant teaches us, can free us from stagnant energy and unnecessary limitations that do not nourish us. Plant is particularly knowing about the void and our need for it because Plant intelligence specializes in guiding animals to what it most needs for growth. Stay in this space for as long as you would like and know you can always come back to the void to let go of stress, pain, outdated beliefs, patterns, and identities that need to be released in order for you to feel calm, healthy, and deeply refreshed. In this way, Plant brings us a way to regenerate through nothingness and begin anew.

While meditating as the void, join me in exploring what prompts the void to shift, resulting in the emergence of the living universe. Plant shares that which sparked life is like the potential within a seed. Imagine the void as dark soil, microbes and bacteria representing invisible intelligence, percolating. Our own consciousness is this seed. We are everything and nothing at once, the non-dual truth of existence. Plant

ONE HEART JUSTICE

embodies this truth by communicating vibrationally, listening to the Source of life. This allows Plant to be fully present within their surroundings as well as firm in their ability to respond to all things from an awareness of achieving homeostasis through constant cycles of birth, death, and adaptation. Plant reminds humans that we often do not have a full picture of our environment or practices that could support us in feeling into how insects, birds, weather currents, sunlight, and microscopic life come together. This is the perspective, and the wisdom, Plant has and uses to guide us.

As I write this today, I am sitting in a mountain town where the cold from the north and heat from the south intermingle to create a temperate forest. Many medicinal plants for humans continue to be rediscovered here, with the support of indigenous knowledge, preserved and shared by local tribes, wildcrafters, and others working to document, discover, and protect the environment. Plants such as ginseng, dogwood bark, and goldenseal have been used for ages and deserve protection from over-harvesting. We must protect biodiversity and remember all plants have purpose. Plant says to look beyond our own species' needs: when we pull weeds or cultivate lawns, we are forgetting about the needs of other creatures.

Plant wants us to know that staying close to the Source of life by feeling love in our hearts as much as possible is an effective way to re-root ourselves as deeply as possible in the universal connection to all things. Plant reminds us that, as animals, we can best share a connection to growing through loving energy. What is Love? Plant says, consider it from the eternal perspective: Love is a force, opening us to understand our connection to everything. From the void, to that original, seed-spark of life, Source disperses itself as Love—perhaps as microparticles we humans have not yet discovered. In this way, nothing becomes everything, and all is, quite naturally, one.

Coming and going into and out of the void, the Source of life exists as an eternal pendulum, swinging back and forth between the full potential of wholeness and nonexistence. Plant is here to help us each personally cycle through this pattern—void, seed, and rebirth—until we are fully awakened, integrated beings, akin to the Tree of Life. The Tree of Life as an archetype in many mythologies and religions represents the spiritual support the universal spirit of Plant has to offer us in connecting to oneness. Our existence is just like the Universal Tree, as we are deeply rooted into the soil (or soul) of Earth. Our spiritual roots reach through Earth into the Source of life. Plant reminds us oneing meditation practice will help us feel our firmly embedded strength as we cultivate and enliven processes to create justice and equity for each other and all of life.

Plant guides us to rise up, rooted in Source, as our body's intelligence branches out, interweaving our nervous systems, hearts, and souls with the Universal web of life.

Plant brings our awareness to fungi as a mycorrhizal network below ground, communicating for the health of the whole community of the forest and other ecosystems. They let us know this is a microcosm of the Universal web of life we are all a part of, and we can give and receive through our awareness of and presence within this state of oneness consciousness. Plant is a model for nurturing community and reminds us they provide medicinal helpers such as mushrooms with psilocybin, that can be taken in a safe and supportive environment as one way to increase our ability to reconnect with the broad scope of Universal presence and the eternal nature of our souls.

ONE HEART JUSTICE

Plant is here to help with the health of our spirit as well as the health of our body. They encourage us each to find our most organic ways of being in modern society while practicing Universal consciousness. This practice of interbeing can lead to mutual support of thriving systems for all humans. Plant says to focus on nourishing our own and others' being toward peace, sharing, innovation, and restoration. How do we do this? Plant encourages us to talk to trees, flowers, fungi, and more as we go about our daily lives. To acknowledge the invisible presence of bacteria, microbes and viruses, and contemplate how they cycle through birth, growth, and adaption toward interdependent diversity. Plant reminds us of our reliance on them through nutrition, medicine, and materials. They let us know that honoring diversity among human beings is exactly what will help us to unlock as-yet undiscovered medicinal teachings and offerings of plants, because honoring each other is pivotal in the development of our ability to read the greater landscape more fully and accurately.

Plant has much more to give us all for revitalizing ecosystems, including our cities and towns. Contemplating and listening to the wisdom of Plant as a spiritual entity, as well as communing with individual plants, allows us to work with them in ways that are beneficial for all. Plants are already responding to humans, animals, insects, birds, soil, water, sunlight, air, and more. They listen in their own Plant ways and grow to meet the needs of all of life.

Plants are highly intelligent creatures that do not experience life and death in the same way humans. "Listen," Plant says, *we know you are afraid and lost sometimes and may even become hopeless about the mess we are in.* Plant shows us that this mess untangles and becomes roots, connecting us with the whole of all that is. Plants, because they are beings, like we are, can give us the tools to tap into the Universal web—through agriculture, land preservation, feeding one another, and using the biodiversity Plant provides to heal one another. Plant sings of biodiversity like a multiplicity of rhymes, multicolored species, phyla, and taxonomies. So much is created in their dense thickets of interwoven nature. When we listen, there is so much to see through loving eyes, in mutual discovery. Plant asks us to take a deep breath and feel it is safe to open our awareness to Universal perception. It can take time to adjust to, and it brings increased joy, creativity, love for life, and wisdom to not be afraid of death but to live life to the fullest. Plant inspires us to increase sharing of information about ecosystems, globally, and to develop whole-planet paradigms of plant communication. When talking and listening to Plant, we develop deeper understandings of how to guide our ecosystems. Plant shares how to engage through ethical practices and mutual respect as intelligent beings.

I ask Plant if I might have an experience of this later today. They show me several of the trees in the places I have lived, the ones that I would visit, spend time with, and honor as friends. Plant wants me to know that trees remember our presence and have an awareness that we are different beings and yet of the same source, and connect to us through our beingness. Plant says, if you listen closely, in a relaxed and discerning way, trees talk to you, as all plants do.

Later in the day, an insect bite on my shoulder that was getting infected, becomes very inflamed. I think about how my body is of Earth and takes part in the interchange of life, in sometimes uncomfortable ways—ways that could end my Earth life, if it were not for the discovery of antibiotics through exploration of mold. Bacteria and viruses, when conceptualized through a holistic lens, push us to work together to coexist and evolve. Often this evolution for humanity involves significant death, which can be very hard to accept. Our love and want for each other to have full lifespans focuses our attention on finding medicines and other forms of treatment to increase survival. I am grateful for the opportunity to take antibiotics to help my body quell this bacterial infection. I am also aware of how our overuse of antibiotics highlights a human opportunity: we can increase systems of wellness and healing to include more Plant-based nourishment. Plant reminds us: sometimes rest, herbal teas and medicines can be enough to bring our bodies healing, in the least invasive ways, and when we need more intensive medicines it is important that they are available for everyone.

Fossil records indicate we have been using Plants for healing for at least 60,000 years. I meditate with Plant and consider the eons of trial and error it has taken to learn about plants that benefit humans, and how this knowledge has been passed down through generations, all over the world. Plant urges us to preserve biodiversity and protect ecosystems from over-harvesting in order to progress further in our coevolution. Continuing to work with traditional healers—documenting their knowledge while preserving the safety of their cultures and land—is a way to move forward ethically. We can continue to use Plant-centered forms of agriculture such as permaculture, combined with scientific exploration of medicines, to coordinate healing with Plant using mutually beneficial practices. The more respect and awareness we have for the protected space needed by Plant to co-create with other animals and elements, the healthier and more balanced our ecosystems become—decreasing the development of interspecies viruses and bacteria.

Plant encourages us to continue collaborating globally as much as possible to discover and exchange information and resources with people and places in need of support. This is especially vital where people are most vulnerable to disease and natural disasters created by lack of resources, helping them to repair or move to ecosystems that are integrated with nature in healing ways. Plant says that global focus and cooperation is needed to stop global warming. If we work together, we can use science—developed with compassion and driven by care for all of life—to continue to change our medical, housing, education, and food systems so that there is more thriving for each person and less struggle. Plant asks us to look deeper into how they interact with other elements and animals to harness missing concepts and practices in our approach to caring for one another in human cultures and societies. A global culture based on the collaborative heart in all beings is our goal.

Plant encourages us to study places like Chernobyl, where ecosystems are reclaiming, and ultimately healing. the environment severely damaged by arguably one of the greatest of human mistakes: nuclear waste. Plant also shares their perception of nuclear weapons—as the most symbolic and dangerous misconception humans have created. Essentially, our mistrust of one another and entrenched belief in dominance has distorted our ability to harness our own capacity for the power of Love. Plant says when we approach each other from a heart-based sensibility—of ourselves and the living world, as nature—we create lasting change for the betterment of all.

Plant gently reminds me it is important for us to develop our understanding of and nourishment of plants that are not intimately important to humans, because they are important to other species. Plant says even humans that study ecosystems do not have a full understanding of how all life forms interact, because the intricacy of details is so vast. Plant says this is okay, and it is helpful to hold a balance of humble empowerment as we develop deeper relationships with the world around us.

I ask Plant about "invasive species"—how humans have unwittingly or purposefully moved plants across oceans. Plant responds with a vision of people coming together all over the globe, in their close communities, to cultivate balance between native and non-native species. Plant shows me the creation of complex ecosystems in our cities and towns, as well as humans creating abundant nature preserves. Agriculture takes the form of small gardens among, within, and on top of all of our buildings. People socialize, nourish, and create by tending to and enjoying the landscapes they protect. Plant playfully calls this period "the great replanting." As humanity becomes an increasingly global community, our ability to focus on local ecosystems from a global perspective is imperative. Plant says we can't go back in time to undo seeming mistakes; we must move forward by learning from the past and listening to native and non-native plants as a guide toward coexistence and flourishing landscapes, both internally and on the ground we walk upon. Plant shares that this vision takes close observation and commitment to connecting with the ways plants communicate. Plant says to imagine evolution a billion years from now, as the Earth most likely reaches the end of its lifespan. What habitats can we create to support the longevity of comfortable human conditions while also caring for other species? What aspects of ourselves and our environment do we want to cultivate, from the perspective of thousands of years forward? Plant says, in a sense Earth is both our parent and our child, as it birthed us and also lives on far beyond what we in our human form will ever know.

Plant asks us to recognize that the electromagnetic information from our heart centers is felt by plants. Plant is nourished by our loving connection, and lets us know that when we attune our, bodies, minds, souls- with the source of life we are sharing in the vibrational language Plant speaks. Plant says we can imagine the presence of Source in all things as a "Universal internet," allowing information and nourishment to flow. Listening to Plant in this meditative state, it shows me that plants grow where they are needed. I see the image of a patch of land with nothing visibly growing. I see myself and the spirit of Plant sitting together on the land, attuning with their presence, and them answering…as microbes, sparkling like stars, are gathering and integrating information and sending out frequencies to plants about what is needed most in that environment. Plant answers and makes their way toward integrated, complex ecosystems, and lets me know that humans do not always understand the organic intelligence of the process unfolding. Plant offers that they understand our current limitations and barriers as people in modern society, and offers to support us in developing the artistry of communicating with plants in simple ways. We can truly care for one potted Plant in our lives to cultivate inter-beingness. We can sit in our city parks, neighborhoods, and yards with the intention of being with the landscape, and allowing it to bring us calm and peace as we integrate the information it shares. Plant says a good place to start in meditation is being with ourselves and the landscape in a state of acceptance and appreciation of how we are in this moment. We can choose to stay in this intention or ask for a vision of how it would be mutually beneficial for plants and ourselves to grow.

In meditation with Plant this morning, it shows me how to communicate with what begins to grow that was held latent in the soil, or finds its way through wind and water to this fertile landscape. I envision integrating research with what I am learning in direct communication with the plants and other elements present. Plant gives me general guidance on how to choose seeds to cultivate, interspersed with what naturally grows. Asks me to consider ways to support insects, butterflies, birds, and squirrels, while also protecting what I grow to feed my family. I see beekeeping and collecting rainwater to support irrigation; tending to annual and perennial plants as well as trees and shrubs, throughout seasonal changes. Plant inspires me to grow more of the food I eat and to cook more often. How does Plant inspire you?

I think back to when I lived and worked on an organic vegetable farm, and long for the vibrant and healthy culture created through working closely with the land—together, laughing, sweating, and getting strong. I miss the potlucks we had, with food made from the fruit and vegetables we grew. I admire how this farm still exists and has evolved over the past 50 years to include community-supported agriculture through every season. The farm kids grew up to focus on land protection, food inequities, and sustainable community. We don't all have to be farmers, but a closer connection to plants and agriculture is healing and inspiring in any way you can fit it into your life.

As I get to know Plant, they guide me to consider the first plants—estimated to have evolved around 650 million years ago. From the mysterious formation of the original cell, to bacteria and then to cyanobacteria, Plant dramatically changed the planet, in large part by releasing oxygen into the ocean, and then, atmosphere. The shift to an oxygen-rich atmosphere is thought to have shifted the planet into a glacial period. Plant emphasizes they have radically shifted the Earth before, and it is essential to reversing global warming that they do so again, by sucking carbon out of the atmosphere, among other benefits. We already know that preserving and planting trees is essential, as is supporting kelp forests, to stabilize our warming planet.

As Plants made their way onto land over millions of years and became more vascular and sturdy, life began to diversify more rapidly. By continuing oxygenation of the planet, and as a food source, Plant spurred the evolution of multicellular, terrestrial, animal life. Plant shares their love for humans and all animal life and lets me know humans are a culmination of planetary actualization. Plant asks us to allow them to take us further in our development by assisting us with reconnecting to awareness of Universal interconnectivity.

Plant lets us know they are an intergalactic presence. As scientists measure light spectra to determine photosynthetic biosignatures on other planets, Plant calls me to imagine far-flung plants of different colors—purple, blue, pink—based on the spectrum of light they absorb. Plants of different shapes, sizes, and colors, not found on Earth, broaden my understanding of Plant as a cosmic force. Plant shares that considering them and other elements in a universal way prepares us toward becoming part of an intergalactic community.

Plant teaches us that transmuting sunlight into food, or photosynthesis, is an expression of unifying collaboration, creating unforetold species. This massive variation of plants, united within the Universal spirit of Plant, guides *us* to feel integrated as unique individuals within a larger whole. Plant wants to nourish us with food and medicine and teaches me that being present with plants involves both giving and receiving. I ask, "What do we have to give to you, Plant?" I hear them call for more wild places to grow, unmanicured by humans.

Plant wants more seed saving, more attention paid to cultivating variation in agriculture through reduction in mono-crops, and an increase in biodynamic structures supporting local rural farms, in collaboration with urban farming. Plant emphasizes that food security and nutritional equity go hand in hand with increasing connection to growing foods collaboratively, as neighbors and community members. We work together to share artistry with foods and cook in ways that deemphasize profit and increase availability through sharing. Plant shares visions of village-style food, focused ecosystems, increasing the benefits of nature in our neighborhoods, whether urban, suburban, or rural, while nourishing our bodies with vitamins and minerals. Plant wants nothing more than to continue supporting the evolution of animals by being more abundant, restored, cared for, and engaged energetically.

As Plants learned to dig their roots deeper by seeping acid into soil, they became stronger, and eventually came the evolution of wood and trees. Trees remind us they are great beings of circulation, weaving an elaborate tapestry, like dendrites and synapses threading new neuro-landscapes through our bodies. Meditating with trees illuminates the flow of our nervous systems and allows Universal integration on a physical and spiritual level. Visiting trees we love, or imagining a special tree and holding image of this tree in our minds, in resonance with our bodies, can support us to harmonize our nervous systems with trees. They circulate loving frequencies, up and down our spinal column, between the Cosmos and Earth. Trees breathe with us to awaken and weave our bodies and souls into a sacred, geometrical web of light and to align with Earth's web of divine life. Trees have also often represented a gateway to other worlds or dimensions of life in many cultures, and are helpful to explore as partners in our meditative journey.

My mediative journey today: I play my drum, sitting in the forest with trees, breathe and Plant shows me a Tree of Life meditation during which each element enlivens one of my energy centers. I feel my heart center radiate as the element of Fire to temper passion as peace to cultivate connection. The Source of life rises through my throat energy center and opens as Cosmos so I may speak with Universal loving intention. Through my third eye center, the Source of life becomes Earth energy, to give me vision and insight toward resonating universally for evolutionary purpose. Up to my crown energy center Water emerges to allow a space to dive in, between spirit and matter and flow with the universal current. The Source of life bursts upward and comes to a rooted place above me, creating an awareness of the channel I am for eternal life. From this grounding in the above, it gently falls back downward, illuminating each energy center again with the Source of oneness and the power of elements: Water, through my crown, Earth, within my third eye, Cosmos, held in my throat, and Fire in my heart. The Source of life then moves downward into my solar plexus, as Air, allowing an organic and humble dispersal of personal power, intertwined with oneness wisdom and equity for all. Moving lower, into my belly energy center, the Source of life is enlivened as Plant, to nourish and be nourished in creative ways. Then to the root chakra, as Animal, deepening connectivity with my human animal drives and enlightening my animal nature with the temperance of eternal abundance and intuitive guidance for just action. Finally, the Source of life descends from my ankles to my feet, the soul of Earth as Light, and deeper still, through the globe into the Deeper Source of life and eternal connection, below. Light grounding by body in connection to source encourages me to express my soul; the source energy vibration of my individual energetic signature or essence. This is one of infinite ways the Tree of Life matrix supports us in human evolution.

It is early fall in the Northern hemisphere, just past the Equinox, and this morning I am cooking with Plant. I practice the One Heart Justice process, put on meditative music, and begin to chop carrots, acorn squash, mushrooms, and garlic. I drink some dandelion tea and feel grateful for this moment in my busy life as a full-time, working parent. I take time to acknowledge my privilege: being able to buy quality vegetables, even when money is tight. For a moment I am moved to tears by the presence of Plant and the beauty of orange carrots, the yellows and greens of squash, and the pungent miraculousness of mushrooms and garlic. Being present with Plant in this way brings me into the power of presence with our everyday world, and how the elements worked together to create humanity and continue to sustain us. It is quintessential to our existence that we emerged largely from the diversity of animal life that plants created, and yet, Plant has become diminished largely in the consciousness of humanity. This is the opportunity of global warming, Plant says to me, in it's ever-gentle way. Plant wants humanity to engage more deeply with it, to listen, to innovate, and to succeed in increasing global harmony and balance for humanity and all of life. Plant again brings me to the concept of roots and restoring ancestral memory. They point to our continued exploration of other beings, such as fairies, gnomes, and other little creatures in our fantasy-based mythology. Plant asks us to be open to the possibility that ethereal spirit beings live among us, most often imperceptibly. They remind us we cannot see most of the processes that sustain us as animals. Plant suggests that we are in a particular stage of human development in which we may rediscover some of the senses we have cast off in the transition to modern rationality and logic. Plant encourages us to grow in our ability to feel comfortable with the experience of other dimensions of reality that we live among and that we are not fully aware of. We are asked to integrate a spiritual sensibility through honoring the complexity of life, and to open ourselves to the loving support of helping spirits. Plant says we each have the choice to integrate ways of knowing that allow connection and exploration of spiritual dimensions in ways that support our understanding and contribution to caring for life on our planet. Plant guides us to be grounded and holistic in our engagement with our spiritual senses. Plant suggests we embody a unified approach, weaving information and experience gained from spiritual contemplation with modern epistemologies.

I recognize that even though I take time to shift into a more focused consciousness of interbeing throughout my day, through the One Heart Justice process or other meditative practices, the experience and insights gained from these moments become part of my being and contribution. I can communicate with the spiritual dimensions of life, including nature spirits, closely aligned with supporting plants, as well as learning through scientific methods and modern technology. Plant allows me to understand more about nature spirits and lets me know they are drawn to places in nature that are wild and diverse because they exist within a frequency of interconnected harmony. Nature spirits support plants by accentuating vibrations of peaceful, creative, and thriving beauty. They nourish plants in an energetic way. Plant says to invite nurturing nature

ONE HEART JUSTICE

spirits to the land you live on by creating spaces they will feel are safe, honoring, wild, and thick with Plants.

I am reminded of when I was 20 years old and studied herbal medicine with a teacher in a mountain forest. I felt the nature spirits connecting with me in their tricky ways to get me to pay attention to expanding my consciousness with Plant. It was and still is challenging for me to share my experience with nature spirits, because it is taboo to acknowledge such things publicly in mainstream modern society. This kind of spiritual acknowledgment comes with a vulnerability to being perceived as delusional, or at least naive and unintelligent. Plant reassures me that the benefits of spiritual wellness through sharing love with nature spirits far outweigh any potential consequences of misperception by other people. I ask Plant to help me understand more about this level of reality on Earth, so closely aligned with the land yet not usually visible. I sense that the variety of spiritual beings living quite differently from humans on our planet are working hard to support our evolution of consciousness. Perhaps humans will evolve to fully witness their plane of existence, enriching our engagement with sacred and powerful entities. Expanding our individual soul/spirits beyond our bodies, with full awareness, helps us to be open to life in its full diversity, interweaving the ethereal and the physical. Plant says, working with nature spirits toward social justice is a unique approach, and that they are harbingers of unity and health. When called to our lands and honored with sacred space, they help cultivate indiscriminate interconnection and energy for creating connective flow through barriers.

Plant asks me to have the courage to share about the Source collective I discovered I am a part of through daily meditation in a sacred forest I envisioned. ...I would enter the forest through my imagination, from a field, through a thicket, into a forest alive with an expanded range of colors—indicating this was a multidimensional experience, outside the human barriers of space time. Everything felt sentient and present to support me. I felt safe, deep; and entered into a transformational process each time I spent time there. When I looked up to the treetops, they formed a heart, welcoming me home. I had many experiences there with helping spirits, and learned much about how to heal old wounds to restore myself to a fullness of conscious interconnection so that I could reflect the Source of life in all things. This is my practice—to give as much as I can through self-love, and sharing support and care.

Among the guiding souls I encountered in my meditative state was a group I considered to be my spirit family of humans—one I had belonged to in the flesh, long ago. With them, I worked through the dynamics of longing and belonging, and other human social dynamics, as they allowed me to feel held, accepted, and honored in my learning. (As I look back at this experience, I realize: I must have processed enough of the learning within my ancestral human body bloodline to perceive my soul family for who they truly are.) As we sat in a circle, around a fire symbolizing the Source of life, all seven of them took off their human exteriors and shared themselves as shining light beings close to the Source of life. From that moment, I have felt my soul family, and every soul has entered the realm of my highest consciousness, and they let me know I am a part of their collective. It has taken many years to integrate the reality of this understanding. I am human as well as an eternal soul, reflecting the light of oneness. I believe this is also true of you, and all beings.

ONE HEART JUSTICE

Over time, my soul family has helped me to understand we are eight beings emerging from and living closely with the Source of life. All of us, and all things, have emerged from this Source and *are* this Source, in limitless form. Living close to the Source of life means we are aware of our infinite selves and work together, sharing loving compassion with all forms of life to harness interconnectivity through Universal Love. This is part of the Universal evolution of life itself.

It is difficult for me to be the only being of my collective in human form. I have to maintain connection with my human family and this space-time sub-point within the Universal whole. Sometimes I worry that I will lose myself in this process no longer be useful to humanity. It is, of course, my heart that allows me to be fully here, human, and present to my life on Earth, as well as part of my soul collective who live in an unembodied, multidimensional state. What grounds me is knowing that all things are of the Source of life, and so when I look into your face, I know we are united in both our humanity and our eternal spirit.

On Earth my soul collective has taken on communicating, for primary intergalactic elements that have culminated in human form, to assist humanity in reaching their fullest potential as the consciousness that interconnects the planet toward the ultimate harmony for Earth. Humanity is more collectively opening to intergalactic kindness and support as part of the process that results in a broadening of intergalactic communication, connection, and harmony. From intergalactic harmony comes Universal harmony, and the Source of life, vibrating at the utmost highest frequency of Universal Love, thereby dispersing into the void of nothingness and rebirthing. This is a psycho-spiritual model of how the Universe expands infinitely, and is everything and nothing, at once. It is, I know, almost incomprehensible. Yet we feel it as humans on some level, because we grow according to this model.

I ask Plant why they want me to tell this story of what I call my soul family in connection with them, specifically? Plant lets me know: this model of growth and trajectory for humanity is like the process of photosynthesis. The sun, as the source of life, is absorbed by Plant and transmuted by a mechanism of their own creation to grow into full expression of all that is and all that can be. It is that fullness that One Heart Justice seeks to cultivate, and Plant shares their compassion for humanity's continued fighting of one another. The fear that holds humanity back is a misunderstanding of the path to fullness. Honoring ourselves, each person, and all of life, allows us to grow together.

Plant shows us the way to find nourishment from the source of life, even in despair and confusion. They say, like the blossoms of flowers, we are beautiful and twinkle like stars. Plant tells me of the resonance between stars and flowers, and that humans are pollinated by light. Natural light, arriving from far-off time, stimulates us to expand our energetic presence and be more fully integrated with the consciousness of oneness. Plant shares this Universal perspective of human growth and asks us to cross-pollinate—through loving one another and caring for ourselves, each other, and the life around us. "Do not be afraid to grow," Plant tells us. Growth as a Universal concept means to be present with the ever-changing internal and external dynamics of existence. It is being present through our integrated realms of consciousness: mind, body, and soul in connection with the spirit of oneness. We are growing now, together, and will continue to discover that Plant is positioned to nurture us in mind, body,

ONE HEART JUSTICE

and spirit toward our fullest expression of the embodiment of Universal Love in this lifetime.

On this sunny day, my awareness is brought to the shadow of Plants, and I think of the psychological concept of the shadow—as aspects of ourselves we have difficulty accepting in wholeness. Plant guides me to embrace these parts of myself, such as difficulty managing anger, impulsivity, challenges with patterns that never seem to change. Plant reminds me I have the choice to embrace these aspects of myself and continue my human personal process of lovingly learning to choose again when I lose my temper or hurt myself or others in some way. We each have choices, Plant says, and self-compassion and compassion toward others support us in stepping out of cycles that keep us stuck personally and collectively.

Plants let us know we energetically nourish them with our awareness and appreciation. We are encouraged by this process to appreciate ourselves and one another. Plant asks us to fully recognize the power this intention and practice has on our personal and collective development. Plant reminds us we can have strong boundaries to protect ourselves and others from those that are hurt in ways that cause them to consistently harm others. These boundaries of love can support more healing over time and illuminate ways to minimize painful dysfunction. Plant also reminds us: human life is full of adversity, and it can nourish us on all levels to endure and transform our individual and communal experiences.

Finally, Plant calls us to imagine a field of wildflowers… and to know this wild beauty as our own, soulful garden, perfect in its natural state.

ONE HEART JUSTICE PROCESS
Universal Heart Meditation

Visit Oneheartjustice.com for guided meditation recording of One Heart Justice process

To begin the Universal Heart Meditation, bring your whole body into awareness and allow whatever needs to dissolve into the void of nothingness to release and fade away. Breathe into this dissolution state and relax into stillness. When you are ready, allow the source of life to emerge through your heart center and breathe deeply into your heart. As you exhale, know that you are in connection with the one source of all creation. Feel your heart spark with the intelligent life force causing it to beat. Allow the spark of life's source to alight in each of your energy centers moving up to your throat center, your third eye center, crown center and up above your head rooting into the source of life. Bring your awareness back down through each energy center and feel the spark of source life energy to blossom in your solar plexus center, your belly center, root center and down into your feet and below rooting into the source of life. Remember you are created of this one magnificent source, illuminating your heart, all of you, and all the innumerable manifestations of creation on Earth and beyond.

From your radiant heart center, and all of your energy centers you can envision and feel this loving source intelligence radiating out from your body, until you are fully residing in a sphere of unconditional love. Stay here for a moment and soak in love as if you are a plant soaking in light.

As you experience the awareness of your whole body within the sphere of universal love, you can allow this energy to continue to expand in all directions, radiating further and further, as far as your sensory awareness and imagination will expand, until you know that you have expanded fully. Feel the love of the universe coming back toward you, enveloping your expansion in a hug, and know that you are fully interconnected with the web of life. From this place, born of the source of all of creation and connected through the force of love, you can begin to listen, ask for guidance, share and receive information.

Hold the spirit of Plant in your heart, your mind, and your body. Be present with whatever arises. As always, if this feels uncomfortable, you may try shifting from fear to curiosity. If you begin to feel overwhelmed in any way, take a break from the practice and engage in self soothing and getting support. When contemplating Plant feels right, continue into Somatic Listening.

Somatic Listening

As you move into Somatic Listening and listen with your whole body by being nonjudgmentally aware of body sensations, images, words, cognitive impressions, and emotional tones, imagine these are ideas allowing you to learn with Plant. If you lose focus, bring your awareness back to you heart center and smile, feeling the presence of Plant in your heart as you breathe and regain focus. Notice what sensations, images, emotions, and words draw your attention most and feel powerful to explore further. Ask Plant what messages it has for you to deepen your understanding of mutual nourishment. Allow the spirit of Plant to illuminate your belly energy center or any other energy center that feels right. As you hone in on impressions to transition into creative exploration with, take a moment to make notes or draw in your journal, or amplify body sensation into movement, or sound. Use whatever ways seem most effective to bring expression and understanding to your Somatic Experience with Plant that is the right way for you today.

Creative Exploration

As you move into the third aspect of the creative contemplation process, Creative Exploration, know that you can return to the Universal Heart Meditation and Somatic Listening at any time, and then back into Creative Exploration.

Your expressive arts practice can be in any artistic medium. You may choose to take your sensory experience into movement, visual arts, sound, or music. You can also focus on a problem you are solving, a current project, a relationship you are in process with and ask Plant to support you with new approaches and ideas. The wisdom you gain in contemplation with Plant is yours to create with in whatever way that is best for you.

Make this experience your own as you move in and out of Universal Heart Meditation, Somatic Listening, and Creative Exploration at your own pace. Be authentic to your own practice and allow your own patterns and methods to emerge. Begin to notice in every day life how Plant is present and how you can sense it as an intelligent force that is familiar in it's connection to your mind, body, and soul.

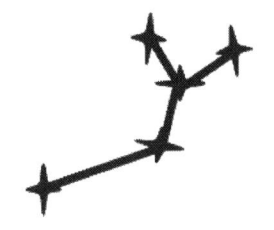

CHAPTER SEVEN

Animal – Take Just Action

"When will our cultural knowledge and our sacredness be as valid as western science, medicine or knowledge."

- Anthony Tamez-Potchel

Animals enliven ecosystems, animating the culmination of elemental possibilities. Comb jellies propel through water, as millipedes walk onto land, tiny, shrew-like mammals scamper among the dinosaurs; millions of years of animal evolution have led to this moment. And, it continues. I am grateful to those who contribute to puzzling out the constantly branching lineages of the animal tree. Within the One Heart Justice process, the Universal Spirit, Animal, asks us to deepen our experience of evolutionary relationships—to let go of traditional taxonomy during contemplation, and strengthen our understanding of animal interconnectivity. Attuning with Animal life allows us to recognize our equal place as human animals among the animals in all of creation. In meditation, we take time to listen directly to Animals we share the planet with and integrate our own experience with information provided by those who have dedicated themselves to studying and protecting various species of Animal life.

Earth has undergone five great mass extinctions; it is estimated that 99% of the four billion species that have evolved on Earth no longer exist. Animal asks us to consider the fact that human choices are causing radical climate shifts, including Animal extinctions, and offers us our collective responsibility: to nurture planetary development. At least 900 species have gone extinct in the last five centuries, primarily through habitat loss caused by human action. Relatively recent extinctions such as the passenger pigeon and the Yangtze River dolphin, caused by overconsumption and pollution, among other human-created factors, point to our hastening of all Animal life toward extinction. What does this mean for human evolution, as we look at our own death mask in the face?

Facing this possibility directly, I sense an opportunity for the falling away or extinguishing of practices not truly essential for our health and development. Animal encourages us to begin by valuing the diversity we ourselves embody, as a guide to restoring the most healthy, nuanced, vibrant, inclusive, and protective environments for each human and for other animals. Honoring diversity, Animal says, leads us to understand ways

ONE HEART JUSTICE

to reweave our cities, towns, and villages within the natural world, to stop damaging practices and reinvigorate health. The One Heart Justice process helps us attune to the source of all as our guide for establishing justice and honoring the wholeness of each being as part of the great beingness of all.

Today, as I connect with the collective spirit of Animal on our planet and beyond in meditation, I sense Animals waiting for more of humanity to connect with them in contemplative, heart-based spiritual communication and visioning. Animal asks us to go beyond our initial responses to our animal kin and to listen deeply to their perspectives, their needs, their ways of contributing to our planet. Through contemplative listening and observation we can generate ways to creatively restore habitat, and in so doing recalibrate our global values. Animal asks us to ground ourselves in deep time and let down the limiting walls of our current conceptual paradigms.

Animal encourages us to value diversity of animal life by collaborating to create safe spaces for growth through the inner workings of respect, support, acceptance, and honor.

From this perspective we find resilience for the challenges of Earthly life and focus on illuminating generative connections for healing our world.

Animal reminds me that one of the greatest barriers to peace within humanity is mistrust. Trust is a moment-by-moment choice we all have available, inside us, to generate safety. I find myself grieving, collectively, for all the ways in which we have betrayed one another's trust. Trust is an aspect of Love, and has the greatest potential to unlock true progress. Trust rings true; it invites the clarity of reflection, empathy, right action and self correction. But what are the motivations for trust-building when it can be so fleeting, uncontrollable, and damaged? Animal states that it takes courage, focus, and perseverance to stay open as well as protected by the boundaries of Love and allow moments of trust to permeate our experience toward a perpetual practice of interrelated growth.

As I sit in contemplation, I recognize the benefits One Heart Justice meditation (and meditation in general) brings to my perception. It helps me to fiercely love myself: my flaws, my gifts, and to own with fullness of heart this human life. It opens me to the absolutely immense diversity and beauty in all things. I am placed in the present moment, which contains within it every moment and is inter-dimensionally informed by all space. The potential we seek is here, and here, in the next, present moment. I share the One Heart Justice process and all contemplative processes to cocreate dynamic loving transformation with other Animals. I realize the power of unified joy, hope, belief, and insight. I realize we each have our calling as we interweave and connect our learning day by day, lifetime by lifetime.

Animal wants us to believe in ourselves as we choose just action. As I sit with this belief, I suddenly feel the weight of intergenerational trauma, the current bloody wars, mass incarceration, poverty, torture, and genocide humanity has perpetrated. I land with a thud, back within the cage of societal cycles of harm. Animal guides me out, with the concept of the unifying spark of the Source of all, present in each aspect of life, enlivening each individual soul and physical presence. We are reflections of one another and are wholly fulfilled when both unified by this Source and interdependently safe through equitable giving and receiving. We are quantum beings: both/and; hurting and healing. Animal says it is time to tip the scales toward healing, to shift the cosmic narrative toward justice and peace. Animal asks us to imagine how we can progress through the sensibility and

ONE HEART JUSTICE

experience of unified living. When weighed down by the reality of our current divisive and traumatized state, Animal asks us to understand our limitless potential for redemption, freedom from fear, compassion, and holding each other up.

I think of all the ways we support one another other and the world around us, and wonder: What prevents us from stopping global warming, extinguishing war, ending poverty, and really moving steadily in the right direction? Animal helps me understand that each person's perspective and voice is like the ringing of a bell. To collectively awaken our understanding of the right path, we can practice listening to one another and integrating information through empathy, distillation of shared needs, and the ability to both take care of ourselves and adjust as needed to support the larger group. In right time, we can continue to forgive each other and ourselves, to restore connection and integrate ways of being that are interconnective. When we are discouraged or in pain ourselves, Animal reminds us that our capacity to listen to ourselves with compassion and encouragement toward healing and growth is essential. Animal remarks at our capacity for renewal on a spiritual level which permeates all of nature.

The One Heart Justice process, among many, supports us in strengthening our reparative imagination. To find ways to honor ourselves and others with the transformative wisdom our hearts provide. We each have the grace of our lifespans to grow in our capacity for empathy for ourselves and each other: to be fierce in loving our own and others' developmental journey; to understand the difference between judgment and discernment; and to fully realize Love's capacity to both keep us safe and provide generosity of spirit for our communities. One Heart Justice practice supports us to stand in the resonance of universal harmony present in the truth of our existence. We can be both uniquely human animals and attuned to oneness as a generative force for healing.

Animal reminds us that healing through the soul and universal spirit is always possible, even as our bodies move toward death. As the animating source energy in Animal life, the Universal Spirit, Animal, helps us integrate the Source of all, with our souls, as both individual and collective beings with deep body knowing. Our heart centers translate Universal Love into energetic presence for our whole selves, and allow our minds to have enlightened purpose. The way of the heart is a path to individual and communal healing. Animal also reminds us that we cannot control or change one another, yet we can create space for the essential components of Love to grow, while at the same time cultivating bio-energetic fields that sieve out energy and actions intended to harm us, as much as we are able. The ways in which we are hurt and harm others are opportunities to heal ourselves and transform the collective. Animal asks us not to dwell in the impossibility that all of our families, neighbors, friends, and enemies will abide by the way of the heart—each being has its own developmental process. Animal calls us, instead, to understand that every individual choosing to heal through love and cultivate harmony with the fundamental aspects of life, ignites inspiration and creates consciousness that lives on. When restoring justice for each other and our animal kin, we are amplifying the threads of the greater web of Universal Love and therefore the Universe itself.

In the One Heart Justice process we seek to restore the marginalized concept of direct communication with animals on a spiritual level and to practice this consciousness with intention for mutual benefit of human and other animals. It is this very

ONE HEART JUSTICE

belief in embodied spiritual knowing through love and heart-based contemplation that has been so threatening to paradigms that only value logic. Animal asks us to be wise enough to reclaim this capacity for heart-based knowing and to reject notions that this subjective experience of life is unintelligent, naive, and disruptive to professional behavior and empirically-based facts. Paradigms that seek to dissuade us from heart-based approaches grounded in ethical consideration and integration of empirical wisdom, are limiting to other ways of knowing that can be integrated with logic and scientific principles.

Animal cautions us not to overthink our way out of intellectual systems of fear, but to shift awareness to our hearts and love ourselves and each other into the next phase of human potential. The dominant, power-over paradigms rely on devaluing others based on classifications controlled by those in power or those seeking to obtain power through violence. To claim the heart of unity, while embracing diversity and staying present with current and historical harm, is the antidote to injustice and creates narratives of collaboration, trust, accountability, innovation, and strength in mutual honor. Animal says do not underestimate the power of unifying principles that actually allowed humanity to evolve to this point. Unifying principles such as intergenerational support, shared resources, respect for differences, utilization of strengths, curiosity and learning brought us to be best of who we are. Our hearts weave stories of inclusivity, belief in human potential, and caring for animal kin.

Animal consciousness on Earth has been traditionally shared through mythology, art, and ritual. The expressive arts component of the One Heart Justice process gives opportunity to directly explore the power and diversity of Animal life. Animal invites us to touch the core of cultural rituals across the ages, designed to deepen our relationships with the interdimensional qualities of animal existence. Human connection with other animals is more than purely physical. It takes on a shapeshifting, intuitive, dreamlike quality, allowing us to develop both our own animal nature and our spiritual capacity for growth.

It is significant that at the very beginning of my daily meditation journey into the spiritual forest, a black bear would meet me at the forest edge, and I would ride on her back along the trail, visiting each place where there was work to be done. In my mind I called to this forest spirit Bear, and she introduced me to my spirit family. My spirit family first presented as part bear and part human, shapeshifters that revealed themselves as beings of light from the non-physical realms. I ask Animal why it was the spirit of Bear that showed me this path. I feel into how bears walk, notice their surroundings, and follow the guidance of their body wisdom. Bear comes forward in my mind and reminds me the One Heart Justice process is about Universal Consciousness, integrated with human, body-based wisdom. Bear calls me to experience my body as an instrument of peace on Earth. Bear shows me that our bodies can be thought of as vibrating wind instruments played by consciously directing Source energy.

As one of many offerings toward creating more planetary peace and harmony, the One Heart Justice process allows for attuning each energy center, like notes of a flute, to radiate Universal Love, creativity, and discovery toward an equitable and thriving world for all. I thank Bear for this guidance and ask both Bear and the Universal spirit of Animal how to utilize concepts such as chakras and spirit animals without compartmentalizing and appropriating different cultures in harmful ways. Animal lets me know this is a delicate balance and one

ONE HEART JUSTICE

that requires us to be grounded in honor and openness to learning from diverse perspectives. I hear Animal letting me know that it is helpful to build trust globally, that sharing and integrating concepts across cultures will support human evolution toward greater unity and health. Animal reminds me: respect, honor, and right relationships happen one step at a time.

I ask Animal: Is the One Heart Justice practice in keeping with this right path? I hear Animal respond: principles of body awareness, alternative states of consciousness, and integrating deep connection between the spiritual and physical dimensions of life are essential for human progress; and we humans can find ways to navigate the bridge between harsh consumption of other cultures and carefully utilizing universal concepts such as body energy centers and the Tree of Life toward increased understanding, support, compassion, and collaboration. I ask Animal to help guide me on this path so that my intention is clear and my communication is humble.

Today, as I am sitting with my own anger and pain related to family dynamics, I feel hopeless about human progress as a whole. Collectively, we continue to turn on each other, denying that all faces are the face of the one Source of life. Long histories of fear, pain, and oppression pass through our bodies, pressing us against one another. Falsity of power allows hierarchies to fuel the illusion of scarcity, as one group forces another to subserve. The spirit of Animal asks us to continue developing our collective support for one another, to transmute grief and rage by strengthening love and hope, as we relentlessly work toward equity and respect. I ask Animal for support in transforming my own wounded heart at this moment, recognizing my sensitivity to challenging group dynamics and my fear and reactivity to my own and other people's misperceptions, reactivity, and anger. Animal guides me to focus on developing the protective boundaries Love can provide. I do this by visualizing a sphere of Love within me and around me, and feel the calming and permeable protection this experience provides. This supports a restabilization of my own inner strength and gives me direction as to how to personally heal my embodied trauma; to become a more healing presence in the world and to get support as necessary.

Connecting to the Source of all through the Universal Spirit of Animal broadens me to consider Animal life on other Earth-like planets within the Cosmos. I wonder how other life forms have evolved and what that could teach us about our own planet. I feel guided to focus on the gift of human consciousness and the potential of transformation within the many ways each person can find healing toward wholeness, through supportive methods of reclaiming a consciousness of Love. Animal emphasizes Love as a universal energy with the power to restore our fullness of existence and lift the wounds of dehumanization. Love is the antidote to fear and the limits fear places on the boundless capacity of spiritual imagination to open channels for equity and solutions to harmful systems, policies, and practices, entrenched in mutual trauma.

I ask Animal, in what ways can humans continue to heal the experiences of traumatic oppression based on concepts of race, class, ability, gender, sexual orientation, and other means of establishing dominance? Animal says humans have the right to choose love over hate and to practice changing their minds and bodies to reflect the clarity of equity and interconnection. The spirit of Animal presents me with the challenging task of not holding hate for groups of humans who bond together through a shared desire for control by damaging others. Animal

ONE HEART JUSTICE

encourages me to let go of hate I hold toward myself for the ways I participate in systems of oppression—as part of the dominant culture in some ways and part of marginalized cultures in other ways. I sit with the fear and confusion of this guidance, afraid to fully let go of hatred, because I believe it protects me from becoming insensitive and keeps me focused on justice. Animal shows me that this hatred I hold onto in secret places of my body and mind is false protection and prevents me from taking full responsibility for the ways I both perpetuate oppression and survive oppression. The energy of hatred is a barrier, and intentionally releasing it from my mind and body creates more space to take responsibility, experience love, listen more openly, and develop more intersectional relationships.

This is why, ultimately, it is a practice of Love and not fear that leads to healing. Fear limits us and binds us to the past. It is Love that gives us courage to transform the past and gestate possibilities to generate more interconnection and inclusive solutions now. The spirit of Animal guides me to focus on the ways humanity continues to strengthen the bonds of Love, empowerment, and shared community to continue shifting ourselves and our communities toward a world that truly works for all. I am asked to share with you Animal's guidance, to find ways to restore our full humanity—meaning, to accept and integrate all aspects of our experience, honoring those who have struggled for us to be where we are today; Also, to understand that by supporting ourselves and each other through difficult layers of healing, we strengthen our bonds and the collective consciousness for human potential. I sit with respect for those who have endured trauma I will never know directly, and commit to continuing my own lifelong healing process to support others in healing. I understand the necessity of collective healing with one another as humans, and with other animals on the planet.

Loving other animals with open intention reciprocates our own healing process. For instance, perhaps by participating in restoration of habitat, we heal our own wounded hearts. Making space for diversity of life inadvertently creates a place to be part of the greater planetary whole, prioritizes safety, thoughtfulness and respect for ecosystems and Animal life. We are more open to other human beings when we practice this generosity of spirit—expanding beyond our differences, and understanding we can honor ourselves and each other with consideration.

Listening to Animal, I hear an invitation for humanity to fully inhabit our awareness of the natural world and reconnect our bodies, minds, and souls to that of which we are made—nature. As humans we are easily lost, hearing only the echoes of our own perceptions within our socially constructed worlds. Animal reminds us it is important to extend our senses to the whole of Animal life on the planet. The Universal Spirit, Animal, asks us to reflect on the loss of animal diversity due to human development, and connect beyond our everyday lives, through contemplation, to the remaining animals in the wild, and to focus on protection. I hear the spirit of Animal pointing to the many illusions humans create and uphold in their hearts, minds, and actions, in order to resist change. Animal calls on humanity to soothe our own fears and collectively evolve to embrace the nature of life and creation as ever-changing. We are asked to have the courage to take on other perspectives and to allow ourselves to imagine what it is like to be another human being or another species, and to value each other in all of our many differences through not only the heart of our shared humanity, but the heart of being alive and in connection with all Animal life.

ONE HEART JUSTICE

The spirit of Animal asks us each to be flexible in our ability to empathize and explore life from a variety of perspectives by listening respectfully to all people and making room for voices of peoples who do not have as much access to forums for sharing their life experiences, wisdom, and needs. We can begin by shining light on our human interconnections and shared living, and extend this relationship to the greater animal community. Just as none of humanity can fully thrive as long as we hold one another down, it is true humanity as a whole cannot thrive on a planet in which Animal life, in the broader sense, is devalued and neglected. At the heart of dehumanization is the ability to detach from the heart of all living things. To fully restore the heart of humanity is to embrace our complex, yet equitable, standing with all of Animal life. The practice of attuning with animals on the entire spectrum of creation will help us to understand and effectively create environments that are most suitable for each person and each animal species, given their needs, gifts, histories, and transformative trajectories toward a thriving future.

Today, as I hold the spirit of Animal in my heart and listen, I hear the sounds of birds chirping, children crying, and the cat purring next to me. I feel the silent abundance of microbes in the soil, the worms slinking in the loam, and I know that soon the cicadas will emerge. Animal reminds me that as individuals we can become so focused on our own lives, we forget how teaming our everyday lives are with the presence of Animal life. Considering animals as animated forms of being, living together and being fed by the Earth and also one another, the spirit of Animal reminds me that the question is not whether it is ethical or not to eat animals, because in one form or another, all of life is feeding each other. It is more a consideration of how we as humans engage in choosing what we eat, how we care for the lives of our fellow animals, and having awareness of how we consume other Animal life. I hear the spirit of Animal telling me that these choices about how to eat and how to kill and prepare other animals are very personal, and we cannot force one another into a single understanding of this. These decisions are for each person to deeply consider, and our choices can be made with gratitude, honor, and respect for all Animal life, and for ourselves as human beings. The spirit of Animal makes it clear that many humans understand that the industry of raising animals for meat production on a large scale is contributing greatly to imbalance on the planet in the form of greenhouse gasses and run-off of pollutants into our water sources. Animal life says that any industry or process driven solely by financial gain will inevitably lead to imbalance for all of life.

We know that this imbalance has grown to massive proportions across Earth, through overfishing and large-scale industrialization of meat and animal product consumption. I am heartened by the many keepers of animals; of cows, chickens, pigs, and fisheries that are truly working toward practices that support all of life. The spirit of Animal encourages me that these efforts are not in vain, and a movement is growing to innovate and restore practices that nourish animals toward human consumption with respect and proper care. Humans are more nourished in body, mind, and spirit when we cultivate systems that are heart-based, sustainable, adaptable, and create wellness.

Imagining periods of human development when we were more often consumed by larger predatory carnivores, it is clear we have found ways to protect ourselves, and Animal life has also changed. Species that have consumed humans for their existence are smaller and less populous, and the spirit of Animal understands why humans have worked together to preserve our families and our lives. Also, we have lost the regulatory balance of not being the top predator, and, along with it, the benefits of understanding the truth that we are not in control of nature. Animal offers appreciation for the knowledge, intelligence, and technology that has come from human study to be used to continue to protect humans, and to focus on efforts of people around the globe who create refuges for large creatures that can cause harm to human beings, as well as creating boundaries that protect other animals and ecosystems from human-made pollutants. Giving space for healthy ecosystems will contribute to preventing an increase in harmful bacteria and viruses, and limit imbalances in species dominance.

Animal calls my attention to the many deaths that are unnecessary in relation to: humans' unequal access to resources; to weapons; gas-powered vehicles; and disease caused by unhealthy environments. Humans have created a far more dangerous landscape for ourselves than other animals ever have. It is helpful to communicate with the spirit of Animal to reorient our values and hone our vision to honor the intelligence and contributions of all of Animal life. Animal reminds me that we can continue to set ourselves apart in our cognitive abilities and use these functions to further understand what is like to be other forms of Animal life. We can contemplate insects, reptiles, single-celled organisms, birds, microbes, and anemones. The spirit of Animal thanks humans who are taking the time to attune with and study the amazing complexity of Animal life on Earth and beyond, to understand the perspective and intelligence of animals that are created by and shape our landscape.

Animal offers a moment to reflect on species that have come and gone, whose existence we have no record of, and to wonder about the value of such creatures who seem to bear no influence on current human commerce. Currently, so many valuable and beautiful animals including the polar bear and orangutan are suffering as their numbers dwindle. How do we repair the distortion of value that has led to prioritizing monetary economies over the wellbeing of large mammals that are so easy for us humans to love? Animal says we need to integrate our Gross Domestic Product with conservation of nature and sustainable systems, in order to heal the disconnect between essentially valuable aspects of life and cultivated currencies derived from entrenched systems of supply and demand that are damaging. Consider that an estimated 5.5 million species of insects make up about 80 percent of all Animal life. This diverse array of tiny creatures, somewhat invisible to humans yet essential to our environments and the food web, has declined by an estimated 40 percent. Reintegrating global value of Animal systems into our societal structures could culminate in the resolution of seemingly intractable human conflicts. Animal reminds me: we truly don't understand the full effect of other animals on the planet. It asks us to be humble and cautious with other animals, and each other. Animal calls us to envision further into the future than our everyday lives allow, to a time when diversity of life can reemerge, proliferate, and continue to evolve in ways that are essential for integrated health.

As I sit in meditation with the Source of life and Animal today, I am urged to share a powerful dream I had a few months ago. It was a dream about the winds of change and the journey toward peace on Earth. As our world transformed, I saw a great burning of current structures. I was alarmed by the raging fires and said in my dream "this is not peace!" It was then the skies turned to blue, and I felt the world become both calm and thriving. I reflect now on the burning fires as the transformation of institutions, systems, and beliefs that have led to unnecessary harm of the environment, humans, and other Animal life. Animal reminds me: we humans have the power of moment-by-moment choices to engage in revolution around our own beliefs, connectivity, and experiences with our world, to guide our planetary journey away from mass destruction. One Heart Justice and other contemplative practices give us the opportunity to renew our perception, focus, and action, as an endeavor in peaceful collaboration. Animal says doing the internal work as individuals to cultivate right action can feel scary, uncomfortable, lonely, and hard. Creating peace is not always blissful; it takes discipline, honesty, hope, support, and guidance. Animal brings my awareness to my heart center as guide, and connects me with the heart of the planet, Cosmos, and Source of life. The heart-based path is the right path if one chooses to be an animal contributing to the healing of all.

We can each practice the most beneficial aspects of what we learn from each other and the living world. Animal highlights our own capacity for redemption and reminds us of the opening grace provides, to work on mutual healing and change. So much of our collective imagination focuses on the exploration of violence, corruption, and mistrust. Animal asks us to understand the power humans hold, in our ability to envision and create narratives of trust with one another. It reminds us, one moment of violence can take generations of healing, and our healing processes are essential to the evolution of our world. Animal calls us to amplify our collective healing and to more deeply explore the possibilities that exist within pockets of peace. Everyday people forgive the unforgivable and restore justice, forging courageous bonds. Humans are not neutral, and so it is imperative we nourish each other with true tales of healing, innovative solutions, and small steps toward bigger changes in the face of the seemingly insurmountable misuse of power. Unconditional love restores the balance of power, and yet it is non-material, only generated by open-hearted intention and disciplined wisdom.

I ask Animal how we might inspire more loving action. I focus on the notion of truth, which no one individual can claim, but reporting of facts can be based on the best assessment of collective information of the time. Commitment to doing as minimal harm as possible can be practiced, as we fiercely learn to do no harm, and to fulfill the requirement of equity of quality of life, for all. Humans are the top of the cerebral Animal apex, so choosing to integrate our minds with our hearts opens us to the unique beings we are, and gives us the ability to be more open to connecting to the core of global humanity and to all Animal life. To connect beneficially to our neighbors and citizens across the globe, we can consider the experience of interconnectivity, cultivated through somatic contemplation and the eternal life energy the Source of creation provides. We can endeavor to hold the Universal Spirit of Animal in our hearts, and commit, one choice at a time, to creating trust and lasting intergenerational bonds among one another.

Animal says we know we are on the right path of collective mindset when we are generous in our perception of ourselves and one another through the universal language of empathy, while at the same time finding equanimity in our own self-loving boundaries. I am all for creating as many bonds as possible through loving wholeness, through creative processes—especially those of One Heart Justice. Animal asks us each to take time, sitting under a tree, to feel into our collective history and the breadth of evolution. Subjugation of self and others, or any form of life, leads to near annihilation of the potential for peace. This form of using fear to over-consume essential resources for an elite population has led us from one genocidal tragedy to another. Animal says we survive through the eternal spark of life that persists and ignites humanity's resilient potential for loving creation. We can't control one another's choices, yet we can inspire them.

Animal asks: *Will you join Me in a dramatic dance of inter-communication toward shared inspiration, information, and actions that heal?* I notice that feeling this empowered makes me feel nervous, like I am doing something wrong and will get in trouble somehow. Animal reminds me the only trouble is being susceptible to responses that attempt to disempower a practice of shared power, resources, and practices for collective healing. I've been hearing the call to be a good ancestor from people partnering for peace, and I resonate with that guidance. We can take the best our familial and collective ancestors have left us—especially the glaring mistakes marking repetitive patterns that are best shifted. We can keep connecting, to self-correct and heal toward best practices, and extinguish power-over drives of aggression with strong infrastructures of shared values.

Animal, in its broad perspective, shares that we, at this point in collective human development, must start with valuing the eternal self, present as each one of us. *We are who we have been waiting for* is a call and response cultures rising from the depths of oppression have passed down through the ages. Self-love helps restore loving perception and connection. It is okay to learn, in our own unique ways, through our own processes, and to support one another through our lifetimes, to the best of our abilities. Heart-based perception allows for generosity, acceptance of self and others and collaborative healing.

Sitting with Animal, today having completed the One Heart Justice meditation practice, I feel guidance to focus on the part of the meditation in which I allow a visceral experience of the void to resolve old wounds from this and other lifetimes. Animal encourages me: *let go of these old wounds and fears, and you will understand, self-love and healing allow for shared love and cultivation of collective healing.* In the face of continued divisive and oppressive power structures, Animal says, use contemplative processes to generate creative community in support of intersectional healing. Animal asks us, in meditative process, to send hope to all Animal species, globally, in order to attune our own personal healing with human communities and all of Animal life. There are enough people who care about one another, other animals, and our whole planet to shift seemingly intractable systems.

Animal asks me to take a moment to feel into our human circadian rhythms and our relationship to darkness and light. Animal offers the concept that light is the truth of being and darkness offers opportunity for transformation. All animals experience lightness and darkness, both as physiological properties of the natural world as well as emotional, psychological, and energetic aspects of collective consciousness. The Universal Spirit, Animal, gives us an opportunity to know as a collective, animal community: we can help one another to go through the challenging experiences of darkness without getting lost. We can restore ourselves and each other to the light of Universal Truth, of beauty shining as each individual being, resulting in the great transformational power of the one Source.

ONE HEART JUSTICE PROCESS
Universal Heart Meditation

Visit Oneheartjustice.com for guided meditation recording of One Heart Justice process

To begin the Universal Heart Meditation, bring your whole body into awareness and allow whatever needs to dissolve into the void of nothingness to release and fade away. Breathe into this dissolution state and relax into stillness. When you are ready, allow the source of life to emerge through your heart center and breathe deeply into your heart. As you exhale, know that you are in connection with the one source of all creation. Feel your heart spark with the intelligent life force causing it to beat. Allow the spark of life's source to alight in each of your energy centers moving up to your throat center, your third eye center, crown center and up above your head rooting into the source of life. Bring your awareness back down through each energy center and feel the spark of source life energy to blossom in your solar plexus center, your belly center, root center and down into your feet and below rooting into the source of life. Remember you are created of this one magnificent source, illuminating your heart, all of you, and all the innumerable manifestations of creation on Earth and beyond.

From your radiant heart center, and all of your energy centers you can envision and feel this loving source intelligence radiating out from your body, until you are fully residing in a sphere of unconditional love. Stay here for a moment and soak in love as if you are a plant soaking in light.

As you experience the awareness of your whole body within the sphere of universal love, you can allow this energy to continue to expand in all directions, radiating further and further, as far as your sensory awareness and imagination will expand, until you know that you have expanded fully. Feel the love of the universe coming back toward you, enveloping your expansion in a hug, and know that you are fully interconnected with the web of life. From this place, born of the source of all of creation and connected through the force of love, you can begin to listen, ask for guidance, share and receive information.

Hold the spirit of Animal in your heart, your mind, and your body. Be present with whatever arises. As always, if this feels uncomfortable, you may try shifting from fear to curiosity. If you begin to feel overwhelmed in any way, take a break from the practice and engage in self soothing and getting support. When contemplating Animal feels right, continue into Somatic Listening.

Somatic Listening

As you move into Somatic Listening and listen with your whole body by being nonjudgmentally aware of body sensations, images, words, cognitive impressions, and emotional tones, imagine these are ideas allowing you to learn with Animal. If you lose focus, bring your awareness back to you heart center and smile, feeling the presence of Animal in your heart as you breathe and regain focus. Notice what sensations, images, emotions, and words draw your attention most and feel powerful to explore further. Ask Animal what messages it has for you to deepen your understanding of taking just action in your life. Allow the spirit of Animal to illuminate your root or pelvic energy center or any other energy center that feels right. As you hone in on impressions to transition into creative exploration with, take a moment to make notes or draw in your journal, or amplify body sensation into movement, or sound. Use whatever ways seem most effective to bring expression and understanding to your Somatic Experience with Animal that is the right way for you today.

Creative Exploration

As you move into the third aspect of the creative contemplation process, Creative Exploration, know that you can return to the Universal Heart Meditation and Somatic Listening at any time, and then back into Creative Exploration.

Your expressive arts practice can be in any artistic medium. You may choose to take your sensory experience into movement, visual arts, sound, or music. You can also focus on a problem you are solving, a current project, a relationship you are in process with and ask Animal to support you with new approaches and ideas. The wisdom you gain in contemplation with Animal is yours to create with in whatever way that is best for you.

Make this experience your own as you move in and out of Universal Heart Meditation, Somatic Listening, and Creative Exploration at your own pace. Be authentic to your own practice and allow your own patterns and methods to emerge. Begin to notice in every day life how Animal is present and how you can sense it as an intelligent force that is familiar in it's connection to your mind, body, and soul.

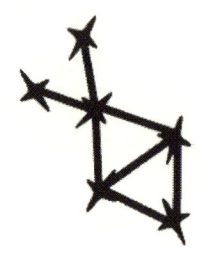

CHAPTER EIGHT

Light – Express Your Soul

"The light of love is always with us."
                                            Bell Hooks

Light can be thought of as an electromagnetic language through which atoms communicate and transform one another. Particles of electromagnetic radiation called photons, created by the birth of the Universe, are predicted to still be in existence when the last star flickers out. Light tells the story of our Universe, possibly even up to its end and rebirth. Current research teaches us that a few hundred thousand years after the

ONE HEART JUSTICE

Big Bang, the Universe was cool enough for atoms of hydrogen and helium to attract free electrons, turning them into neutral atoms; photons were able to rest, and began to travel freely as the electromagnetic radiation we call Light. Stars, galaxies and eventually homo sapiens were created—as photons move in and out of atoms, creating new molecules, one aspect of life creates another. These photons, this energy, the electromagnetic radiation, Light, is another way the Cosmos is interconnected as a Universal whole. As the child of matter and antimatter, Light reminds us life manifests from the unmanifest and communicates through the electromagnetic vibration of our beingness.

Contemplating Light, as a universal entity communicating vibrationally between all forms of life supports our awareness of interbeing. Experiencing inter-beingness through somatic communication with Light can expand our ability to perceive Light as both visible and invisible electromagnetic information moving through the neural network of the Cosmos. Allowing our heart-based awareness of Light to permeate us provides an experience of Universal Love and interconnectivity that supports choices to further integrate human systems with natural systems and better support the whole of existence on Earth.

Each being or aspect of life emits an electromagnetic frequency that can be perceived as an individual expression within the whole. On this late fall day, Light guides me to stand in the sunlight and soak in the warmth of the sun. Light communicates with me in this contemplative moment that expanding our perception of sunlight to include the transmutation of atomic energy into Universal Love can be like experiencing photosynthesis through somatic imagination, for the healing of humanity. . .. *On the other side of existence is nothingness, I feel into this space of no space, and each time seek the truth of* what sparks life. I may never fully understand, yet the practice of exploring nonbeing becoming life is always renewing. I get a sense of being nonexistent, then surrender and release. When I'm ready, I allow Source energy to fill my body, feel connected to the Cosmos and simultaneously aware of the other side, nonexistence. I sense multidimensional realities coming in and out of existence as emptiness becomes aware of itself.

Connecting to Light in all wavelengths as the energy of Love opens us to possibilities held in the communicative power of Light. Listening to Light brings me to my heart center and the electromagnetic radiation my own heart emits. We can think of the electromagnetic radiation of hearts as the Light of Love. Many aspects of major religions and spiritual ways of life call us to the core of the heart as a gateway to the engagement and expression our true self. Just as the right balance of Light opened paths for humanity to eat, live, and produce in ways that drove the development of our species, so Light now calls us back to the core, allowing us to let go of what is not necessary, to preserve a place of essential interconnection. What does it feel like to be more authentic, soul-oriented, and heart-centered?

Light encourages us to heal and grow into the presence of our souls by practicing non-dual, conscious awareness of being both an individual being and unified with all that is: both wave and particle. The soul is a unique composition of existence, individual in its design, expression, and evolution, while simultaneously functioning in harmonious activity as part of the greater whole. Contemplation with Light brings me an understanding of the soul as the unique spiritual signature or eternal energy body enlivening each being. Light encourages us to experience the power and purpose of our souls by shifting from our mental cognition into a presence of embodied intelligence. We sense

ONE HEART JUSTICE

the soul, we know when we are being soulful, when our soul is moved. The soul can be understood as the deepest essence of our bodies and minds, integrated with our timeless consciousness. Our souls may be the truth of ourselves entering this lifetime and going on after we die. Light offers us a process to more deeply experience and express our souls, and wants us to know our soulful presence is important and makes a vital difference in the energy we share with all of life. Each being is welcomed to become more aware of existing as a unique vibration, or Light source of cosmic information; part of all of creation.

Cultivating our awareness and expression of soulfulness is a wonderful way to honor our precious lives and the spirit of Light. Light says, believe in your eternal energetic presence and the wisdom held in your soul. To begin enlivening our souls in new ways Light reminds us to sit in a meditative state with the awareness of our whole being and understand that our core selves are the presence of our beingness beyond aspects of personal identity, and to experience ourselves, even beyond the time and space or historical period we currently exist within. To practice experiencing our pure beingness as our core or true selves provides energetic healing; letting go of aspects of self that we have outgrown or do not fit with who we are becoming. In somatic meditative process, sitting with the truth of our beingness, it is more possible to experience fullness of universal connection. What we experience as our core selves can blossom through the support of Light meditation, toward our luminously integrated soul or eternal energy body, interconnected with our physical bodies.

Light is a great teacher for accessing levels of beingness toward a more soulfully embodied and empowered life, because its universal gift is the integration and communication of the eternal energetic presence of matter. Light wants us to utilize this gift through somatic contemplative processes, including the One Heart Justice process, to support us in accessing our soulful presence, our universal selves through our heart centers. Light calls us to practice feeling our soul bodies through interoceptive focus, guided by its support. How does Light support you in identifying and grounding into your own soulful presence? This rich, vital body of knowing seeks truth and resonates with the souls of all beings who have an innate understanding of the infinite and the one.

Light supports us in honoring our soul's wisdom, so that we may walk together as Universal beings of eternal Light, contributing to Love within life on Earth. Following the resonance of soulful knowing, we continue to grow and evolve as the wholeness we are and can share our unique expressions in unifying ways with each other and all that is.

Light also generates awareness, revealing methods of using Source life energy to transform global systems for equal distribution of resources. The Universal Spirit, Light, offers that it is possible to unite the global economy with Universal life energy through the flow of love in our everyday conscious actions. Light acknowledges this may seem inconsequential and reminds us that our individual practice of choosing to give and receive through the current of Universal Love supports this transformation. Light asks us to empower ourselves by taking the time to visualize vital resources such as food, water, housing, healthcare, and access to education as being distributed with ease to all peoples, in the same way that Light provides consistency for information and nourishment. Light reminds us: global resources are meant for all of life on our planet. Each person has a choice to connect with the guidance of their own

ONE HEART JUSTICE

heart center to generate ways to give and receive, in balance, toward creation of health for all. Engaging in contemplative practices to connect the electromagnetic frequencies of our heart centers and the light of our own bodies with the frequencies of Light is one way of contributing to the larger field of compassion and respect. This field has the potential to reweave currents of resources held in pockets of fear and power. Our individual choices and practices contribute to peaceful means to encourage each other to share privilege and power so that all may thrive. Light understands that this may seem like an impossibility and supports us in taking a leap of faith to embody this knowing, so that within our own consciousness we are integrating the flow of Universal Love with the current of the human economy. Light shines truth on our economic systems, revealing great swaths of misrepresented value. The One Heart Justice process and other contemplative practices give us the opportunity to restore the truth of equal value for all people, all other animals, plants, water, air, fire, the whole of Earth and the Cosmos itself. Moving from the micro: individual embodiment of the light of truth in oneness; to the macro: interconnectivity of the living universe, allows the generative power of consciousness to unite the flow of resources with the flow of Universal Love.

We are asked by Light to connect our heart centers and open all of our energy centers to the information Light has to bring to our body and soul. As reflections of the Light of oneness, our beingness can become more fully enlivened by meditating with Light. Light reminds me it is this illuminative experience that supports healing the wounded parts of ourselves and others, within the legacies of intergenerational trauma. Self-guided, somatic-based meditation does not take the place of professional mental health support, and it is important to get professional treatment for trauma-based challenges. When it feels right, one can engage in self-healing in safe and sensitive ways.

Contemplation with the Universal Spirit of Light can also provide support for bringing a heart-centered approach to community healing. We can embody the Universal truth that we are all souls inside a shared humanity, while we each take our unique responsibility for the way our shared histories of dehumanization and power imbalances intersect. Light guides our contemplative creative processes, through visualization and somatic experience, to provide us with strength, compassion, and clarity to restore us to the fullness of our true selves. An embodied sensation of healing light allows us to witness our personal and collective histories more accurately. We are able to digest the origins of our current issues and find compelling guidance for processes that restore the truth of justice, within inter-beingness. The core wounds that culminate in policies reinforcing poverty, inequity in housing, reduced access to education, food insecurity, and lack of resources for health and safety, lead back to legacies of dehumanization. Light asks us to contemplate paths to equity through respectful connection and to start by shedding our internalized fear about our own organic, true nature.

Self-love is a radiant force; it nourishes Source energy and emerges as our beingness in unique patterns we call our soul. Our beingness is Source life energy, and Light is energy information, evoking our soul's intelligence about the field of energetic connection we exist within. Light offers us the opportunity to shift from our minds into the knowing of our souls; to orient toward our eternally transforming selves. Balancing our human bodies and functioning with the perspectives of soulful presence can provide an expansive foundation to act, moment

ONE HEART JUSTICE

by moment, for healing and respectful engagement with all. Bonding with Light, our embodied sense of self as the source of life becomes more visceral, and our souls unite us with the Universal flow of Love. Love is the interconnective state of all things. So, when we bond with Light in this way, we create an opportunity for infinite healing. When our sense of self is hurt emotionally, psychologically, and/or physically, we can find recovery and renewal by restoring experience of our universal self as an expression of Source energy. Renewal and redemption are possible through the ever-present energy of Universal Light, delivering the healing frequency of Love.

As I join with Light today, I am hurting. My whole-body aches, and I don't know why. I ask the Source of life to help me feel healing and peace, and a Great Heron comes and lands beside the canal trail I am walking. Struck by the presence of the heron standing in the light by the water, I allow myself to grieve for the beauty and temporal nature of terrestrial life. I feel my aging body; Light reminds me I am part of eternal nature. To be in touch with Universal Love in this moment is to find peace and allow my true self to shine fully—to feel Source energy in all forms. Light, as Universal Love in energy form, shows me how to restore myself.

Visualizing Light energy in our bodies can support us in releasing patterns, beliefs and memories that do not resonate with our fullness of health. Light as energy created by the material world can be thought of as a bridge between the spirit realm and consciousness held in our physical bodies. Our bodies generate light waves outside of our visual spectrum. On a walk, communing with Light, I feel the light of my body connect with the great expanse of the electromagnetic spectrum all around me. I set my intention to attune to the Light information that will bring the most love and healing to myself and the world, and I trust that my consciousness will be drawn to and informed by Light as I reconnect with this intention throughout the day. In this way, Light begins to teach me about giving and receiving. Love is the interconnective force formed from the nothingness that birthed all that is, and Light provides a way to harness Love in the form of transformative frequencies and energetic transformation.

The dual nature of Light as both wave and particle reflects the paradoxical essence of life itself as both beingness and nothingness. Cultivating a visceral understanding of this truth supports us in feeling our humanness within the greater context of existence. Filling ourselves with this consciousness provides us with the ability to be strong in our generosity, compassion, and ability to embody justice—being vocal and informing our actions with these qualities.

Light communicates we each have a soul that existed before we were born and continues when our human bodies die, and we have the choice to use our expanded state of being for the betterment of life on Earth, using the oneness principle as our guide. I ask Light to help me understand the soul in a new way. Light shows me our souls are made of eternal essence, invisible to our current categories of substance. All matter comes from this essence as a microcosm of existence. Our souls animate our bodies, illuminating our unique life energy in physical form. Our souls carry wisdom information from other experiences that can inform us, through a sense of knowing, and, when our souls leave our bodies, we regain awareness of our expansive, cosmic lives. Light allows me a glimpse into this remembrance and reminds me, during this human life, to focus on allowing Light to bring awareness to my own layers of beingness. Light reminds me its interactions with matter created the structure of the Universe, and it can be connected with, in meditation, to activate our soul—our deepest connection with existence—which radiates as our true self. Our true selves can be thought of as our individual souls in full expression, through our bodies and in connection with the Source of all that is.

Soul-based activism, or moment-by-moment action can take many forms, and shifts the current notion of activism and radical change into a realm of sustainable justice-seeking, so that we resist becoming the forces we work to transform.

Our heart centers are like the origin of existence, the center from which all emerges and returns. Light says that our true selves can become muted or hidden from awareness by temporal experience and trauma held in our bodies, and offers that the fullness of our true selves can be restored through contemplative practice with Light. Developing a sense of our true selves shining fully through our bodies is a somatic process that can transform damaging thoughts, emotions, and memories, and allow us to let go of painful limitations while accepting what is essential for our personal soul learning. Light encourages us to explore and increase the flow of Source energy through all the layers of ourselves and the Cosmos. Expansive, clear, and flowing energy centers allow for more interdimensional wisdom, which, Light offers, will support each of us in maximizing our lifetimes on Earth and increasing our interdimensional awareness, profound empathy, and new connections for healing and growth. As science moves closer to using fusion to create non-carbon-emitting energy, Light calls us to understand that cultivating our own and each other's personal energy signatures, through careful connection, is also vital to planetary healing.

Light again brings my awareness to my heart center and the power of Universal Love that is available to connect with other hearts. The power of our heart centers can open doors of interconnection, and visions for ways of being, far removed from the seemingly insurmountable problems of the age. It is the eternal flow of life, Light communicates, that carries us to where we most need to go, to hear, to do, and to be. Trust in Light as energy information, fueling the Universe and threading the paradox of everything and nothing that is—into oneness. Focusing on Light nourishing our souls as an expression of our most authentic and whole, true selves is an enlivening process that activates the most intricate and unique patterns we carry to contribute to our world. To nourish our souls with somatic-based Light meditation is a practice directly aligned with developing human potential. Light shares that as we practice shining our own true selves—or souls—we inspire others to do the same. This is one-way human consciousness can evolve, inside the power of complexity of beauty, for increased acceptance, honor, and harmony. This morning as I meditate on Light nourishing my soul, I feel it drawing my soul to inhabit my body more fully. My practice of meditating on physical healing with Light is allowing my soul to inhabit my body more fully. This fullness is energizing; I feel a new sensation in my fingers, and my toes, and just outside my body. The core of who I am is expanding throughout my body to the edges of my physical being and beyond, and all of me is aware of my resonance with the invisible fabric of Source, connecting all things. Light encourages me to continue attuning to it for support in activating my eternal body and noticing how this process informs my day.

I have learned a great deal about my soul today, from intermittently becoming aware of Light awakening my understanding of how the soul functions. Light shows me all that is, and the nothingness from which existence emerges, as a united field, beyond the subatomic level. I feel all of life transforming, in and out of nothingness, moving in infinite directions at once. My soul longs to return to this field of expansive unity. From this, all is created, moving through kaleidoscope formations as expressions of oneness that can be thought of as the souls inhabiting all natural life, connected to the Source of creation. Today was the Solstice in the Northern Hemisphere, and I think about the binary of light and dark. Light wants me to know that even when the visible light of the sun is not present, the life-nourishing presence of Light can be felt. As my soul inhabits my body more fully, my interoceptive sensation feels more whole and changes my experience of presence. I am a soul, inhabiting my body in connection with all that is and interacting with other souls. This orientation as a soul in a body, as opposed to a body that contains a soul, allows me to feel more grounded, strong, and able to move through life in mutually beneficial ways. Light encourages me to imagine and feel Light energy soaking into my soul. I viscerally sense and have a vision of my soul as my eternal body connected to my physical body in this lifetime. Light teaches me that my awareness has an illuminative power. My awareness and imagination merge into a felt sense of healing with the energy of Light. The concept and experience of the soul remains both mysterious to me and also is more real in my present-moment experience. In this process of adjusting to the felt presence of my soul encompassing my body, I notice my body is afraid to let go of the ways it holds tension in an attempt to control life. Shifting to soul awareness feels uncomfortable at first, and I ask Light for guidance. I am filled with focus, and keep gently reorienting myself to the expanded presence of my soul encompassing my body. With practice, I am able to feel more grounded and aware, and less physically sensitive to stress.

Over days of this practice, I feel able to allow my soul to feel connection with all the souls around me, in a way that speaks to the unity and uniqueness in all of life. My orientation to other beings shifts, and I have a deeper sense of honor, curiosity, and love for each person, each soul's presence and lifetime. Soulful presence, meditating with Light is bringing me a sense of peace toward my own life, the hurt I've caused and endured, and the pain and struggle of learning as a human. I begin to take time to daily imagine Light—from the beginning of the manifest Universe, onward—enlightening my soul. I feel stronger, less prone to anxiety or dissociation in difficult moments, and resolved in what I feel called to give and receive. I also notice, one day during my meditation with Light, a place of physical pain in my back, heart center area. I ask for Light's support in understanding how to resolve this pain. It shows me the ways I hurt my younger brother with my anger as a child, and I am drawn to honor his beautiful soul, from birth to now, and send him love for healing. As this pain begins to shift, I am also brought to guilt and sadness regarding other souls' lifetimes, and the hardship, shortened lives, and pain others endure. I ask Light to help me understand how to hold this reality on Earth.

Light asks me to let go of guilt and feel honor toward others who have challenges I personally have not had to bear. Light reminds me humanity is a collective, and it is most helpful to experience empathy and cultivate my own health in order to offer support to others. What one of us experiences is the responsibility of all of us. Choosing to focus our intentions as a united entity on the planet will support us in our collective evolution.

ONE HEART JUSTICE

Light inspires us to understand *it* as a model of the way our consciousness moves through space and time; that is held through the unifying aspect of our soul, over lifetimes, throughout the Cosmos. It offers us wisdom to take the long view, as ancestors to those who will live thousands of years from now. Light gives us hope to shift from our dystopian fears and encourages us to imagine we are nourishing each other's souls and cultivating our own, toward a better future for humanity and for all life forms on Earth—and in the greater Universe, beyond what we are aware of at this time. Contemplation with Light allows us a sense of the invisible intercommunication happening all around us. Light asks us to attune to the electromagnetic experiences of compassion, innovation, courage, and beauty; to stay open to nurturing aspects of human experience that will lead to increased balance, unity, and harmony. Light shows us how to illuminate our souls and to live from an embodied awareness of our own Universal energy, and accumulated consciousness. As we shift from our social identities—based on the concepts of the time periods and places we live in—to a personal experience of soulful presence, we can become even more grounded in expansive, strong, and purposeful existence, rooted prior to and beyond our current life span. Light offers us this practice, because the quality of the electromagnetic spectrum is one of dynamic intersection, both created by and able to create matter. Light holds truths regarding the possibility of the impossible—one particle existing and not existing simultaneously—the same, yet entirely different, as a wave. Light shares collective human consciousness, holds this potential for transformation, asks us to invite Light into the levels of our beingness to support an awakening of our soul awareness.

As I become more soul-aware and feel a glowing light body of consciousness throughout my physical body, I am able to connect more fully to the Universal consciousness of all that is around me. It supports me in tolerating the limitations of my animal body and to feel more honor and integration with other human beings, animals, plants—all forms of life. I am able to experience human-made objects for the intelligence of the elements they are made of, and further sense that they can continue to be transformed in ways that support the whole. Attuning with Light helps us grow in our understanding and ability to create more integrated and wholly beneficial ways of living within the planet.

Light travels 671 million miles per second and carries information faster than any other form of energy we are fully aware of. All things created and destroyed in the Universe as we know it are always present and traveling within space-time. Light shows us how to fully integrate with all that has been, all that is, and all that will be, by fully being in our soulful presence. Though we do not understand what consciousness is made of, necessarily, we can explore the notion that our eternal bodies model Light in the way it continues on, follows certain principles, and holds information that is important for the collective. We know the Speed of Light is possible because Light itself brings us this information. Light encourages us to ask our souls what else they have to tell us that will be of most use to bringing more equity, balance, and love-in-action to our planet.

In contemplation with Light, it reminds me the most important currency for shared wealth is Love in the form of compassion, respect, sharing, forgiveness, and honor. Light would like to support more humans in experiencing the possibility of giving and receiving, through actions fueled by the heart.

ONE HEART JUSTICE

Cultivating grateful and generous hearts happens one gesture at a time and transforms each of us when we experience it in unique ways, just as different frequencies of Light engage one another and shift. To help others heal and reclaim their soulful presence is vital, on both the individual and collective level. On an individual level, simply shifting our body language to convey caring, and establishing trust by acting on that care, is effective. On the collective level, policies and systems generating reparations create fertile ground for mutual thriving in ways that increase health for everyone and everything.

As human animals, our circadian rhythms are affected by natural patterns of Light. We only see a small spectrum of all the wavelengths traveling through space. When contemplating with Light, one can feel its care for us as humans. It asks us to collaborate, caring for our own health and the health of all of nature, by reducing light pollution and creating living and working structures that harness the wellness characteristics of Light. Technologies that reduce damaging environmental impact while maximizing healing communication and preserving nourishing environments through balanced and thoughtful methods are priority.

As the electromagnetic language of existence, Light reminds us it communicates with all beings in purposeful and unique ways. Light reaches out during meditative inquiry and other distinct moments, to say it has much to teach us about enlivening our soulful presence; about contributions and processes to support our individual and collective human development. Light offers information to utilize its properties further—for communication, transportation, food creation, and habitat renewal.

Light offers that it is soulful presence and awareness, and it can best synthesize the electromagnetic information available at any given moment and help us determine the most healing next step for all. Allow Light to hold you gently in the frequency of the Source of Oneness. Know our souls have important access to it, to generate ways of creating the workable infrastructure and lived experience of Oneness on Earth.

ONE HEART JUSTICE PROCESS
Universal Heart Meditation

Visit Oneheartjustice.com for guided meditation recording of One Heart Justice process

To begin the Universal Heart Meditation, bring your whole body into awareness and allow whatever needs to dissolve into the void of nothingness or empty space to release and fade away. Breathe into this dissolution state and relax into stillness. When you are ready, allow the source of life to emerge through your heart center and breathe deeply into your heart. As you exhale, know that you are in connection with the one source of all creation. Feel your heart spark with the intelligent life force causing it to beat. Allow the spark of life's source to alight in each of your energy centers moving up to your throat center, your third eye center, crown center and up above your head rooting into the source of life. Bring your awareness back down through each energy center and feel the spark of source life energy to blossom in your solar plexus center, your belly center, root center and down into your feet and below rooting into the source of life. Remember you are created of this one magnificent source, illuminating your heart, all of you, and all the innumerable manifestations of creation on Earth and beyond.

From your radiant heart center, and all of your energy centers you can envision and feel this loving source intelligence radiating out from your body, until you are fully residing in a sphere of unconditional love. Stay here for a moment and soak in love as if you are a plant soaking in light.

As you experience the awareness of your whole body within the sphere of universal love, you can allow this energy to continue to expand in all directions, radiating further and further, as far as your sensory awareness and imagination will expand, until you know that you have expanded fully. Feel the love of the universe coming back toward you, enveloping your expansion in a hug, and know that you are fully interconnected with the web of life. From this place, born of the source of all of creation and connected through the force of love, you can begin to listen, ask for guidance, share and receive information.

Hold the spirit of Light in your heart, your mind, and your body. Be present with whatever arises. As always, if this feels uncomfortable, you may try shifting from fear to curiosity. If you begin to feel overwhelmed in any way, take a break from the practice and engage in self soothing and getting support. When contemplating Light feels right, continue into Somatic Listening.

Somatic Listening

As you move into Somatic Listening and listen with your whole body by being nonjudgmentally aware of body sensations, images, words, cognitive impressions, and emotional tones, imagine these are ideas allowing you to learn with Light. If you lose focus, bring your awareness back to you heart center and smile, feeling the presence of Light in your heart as you breathe and regain focus. Notice what sensations, images, emotions, and words draw your attention most and feel powerful to explore further. Ask Light what messages it has for you to deepen your experience of being an eternal soul in human form. Allow the spirit of Light to illuminate your feet and the energetic center below your body. Allow Light to activate any other energy center that feels right. As you hone in on impressions to transition into creative exploration with, take a moment to make notes or draw in your journal, or amplify body sensation into movement, or sound. Use whatever ways seem most effective to bring expression and understanding to your Somatic Experience with Light that is the right way for you today.

Creative Exploration

As you move into the third aspect of the creative contemplation process, Creative Exploration, know that you can return to the Universal Heart Meditation and Somatic Listening at any time, and then back into Creative Exploration.

Your expressive arts practice can be in any artistic medium. You may choose to take your sensory experience into movement, visual arts, sound, or music. You can also focus on a problem you are solving, a current project, a relationship you are in process with and ask Light to support you with new approaches and ideas. The wisdom you gain in contemplation with Light is yours to create with in whatever way that is best for you.

Make this experience your own as you move in and out of Universal Heart Meditation, Somatic Listening, and Creative Exploration at your own pace. Be authentic to your own practice and allow your own patterns and methods to emerge. Begin to notice in everyday life how Light is present and how you can sense it as an intelligent force that is familiar in it's connection to your mind, body, and soul.

Works Cited

Noonuccal, Oodgeroo. *My People.* New Jersey: Wiley, 5th Edition 2020. Print.

Childre, Doc., Howard Martin., Donna Beech., *The HeartMath Solution: The Institute of HeartMath's Revolutionary Program for Engaging the Power of the Heart's Intelligence.* San Francisco: HarperOne, 2000. Print.

Harjo, Joy. *In Mad Love and War.* Middletown: Wesleyan University Press, 1990. Print.

Butler, E. Octavia. *Parable of the Talents.* New York City: Grand Central Publishing, 2000. Print.

Clifton, Lucille., *The Collected Poems of Lucille Clifton 1965 – 2010.* Rochester: BOA Editions Ltd., 2012. Print.

Nhat Hanh, Thich. *Present Moment Wonderful Moment.* San Francisco: Parallax Press, 2022. Print.

hooks, bell. *All about love: New visions.* New York: HarperCollins, 2000. Print.

Anthony Tamez-Potchel is a First Nations Oji-Cree/Black activist working toward collective liberation. Learn more at anthonytamez.com

Made in the USA
Middletown, DE
22 July 2024